STOKE CITY
On This Day

STOKE CITY
On This Day

History, Facts & Figures
From Every Day of the Year

RICHARD MURPHY

STOKE CITY
On This Day

History, Facts & Figures
from Every Day of the Year

All statistics, facts and figures are correct as of 31st August 2008

© Richard Murphy

Richard Murphy has asserted his rights in accordance with the Copyright, Designs and Patents Act 1988 to be identified as the author of this work.

Published By:
Pitch Publishing Ltd,
A2 Yeoman Gate,
Durrington BN13 3QZ

Email: info@pitchpublishing.co.uk
Web: www.pitchpublishing.co.uk

First published 2008

10-digit ISBN: 1-9054113-1-6
13-digit ISBN: 978-1-9054113-1-3
Printed and bound in Great Britain by Cromwell Press

To those who brought me here in the first place:
my father, John, and my grandfather, Pop.
Thank you both.

Richard Murphy – September 2008

FOREWORD BY NICK HANCOCK

From a personal point of view, it is particularly fitting that this fine book has been presented in the form of a diary because I think about Stoke City every single day: 365 days a year (and, on occasion) 366. Stoke City digs me in the ribs and reminds me of some fantastic, or terrible, moments I have enjoyed or endured in the near 40 years I have been following the team.

Some days I'm with my Granddad pounding my feet on the wooden floor of the Butler Street Stand as Harry Burrows, Terry Conroy or Jimmy Robertson hurtle down the wing. On others, I'm trying to control my excitement at a hostile Roker Park as Brendan O'Callaghan nicks the game with a last minute header.

It's unsurprising really, especially when you consider that my house is full of the most incredible amount of Stoke City tat; from an early seventies Stoke City comb case (yes they existed), to a set of Russian dolls in Stoke kit comprising in descending order: Clive Clarke, Carl Asaba, Ed de Goey, Darel Russell and (brilliantly) tiniest of all, Dave Brammer.

I don't mind it of course, and many's the time I have a little chuckle to myself, out of the blue, about some brilliant away trip to Hull or Carlisle, Ipswich or Brighton. The club punctuates my life and the games are little flags in my own personal history. I could probably write a personal 365 day diary of Stoke City memories but for now this excellent book is providing distraction enough.

Nick Hancock

Incidentally both the first and last paragraphs of this foreword have 72 words, and 72 is a key number for Stokies. A sad observation but that's the way it gets you!

INTRODUCTION

Stoke City: On This Day is a journey through the year with the history of the club as your travelling companion. The book is packed full of facts, figures and trivia from Stoke City FC's history for each and every day of the year.

The great sides of the 1940s and 1970s are here with tales of title challenges; so near and yet so far. The cup runs with final joy, and semi-final despair, are here too. The book dabbles – as has the club – with European adventures and exotic end-of-season tours. There is room for the great players to have graced the club: Matthews, Banks, Hudson, Hurst, Steele, Franklin, and Greenhoff. The managers are here too from the long-serving legends to the brief failures. The great signings, the goalscoring feats, the amusing anecdotes, it's all here. An opportunity to look back as the club looks forward to the future.

I would like to extend my thanks to everybody who has had a hand in putting this book together. To my editor Dan Tester at Pitch Publishing, thanks for the advice and patience in the completion of the manuscript, it was one hell of a learning curve, and everyone else at Pitch who has had a role in this.

To all of those at Hanley Library and Stoke City Football Club who have assisted when necessary, I thank you for your detailed knowledge. To those who have previously written books about Stoke City – Simon Lowe, Wade Martin, and Tony Matthews – thanks for the hours of reading.

Thanks to Nick Hancock for agreeing to write the foreword. To those who have shared the joy, pain and emotion; on the terraces and in the stands; past, present and future; we went through it all together. Thanks to my mum, Freda, for helping out when called upon. Last, but certainly not least, thanks to Naomi for her love, her assistance and for doing without me for a while. She now knows more about this football club than she ever thought she would know or ever wanted to know.

The research for this book has been pleasurable yet strenuous and I have spent many hours knee deep in programmes, newspaper archives and the books of Simon Lowe, Wade Martin and Tony Matthews. I hope you get as much pleasure reading this book as I did from compiling it.

Richard Murphy, September 2008

MONDAY 1st JANUARY 1906

Tom Holford became the first Stoke player to appear in 100 consecutive league matches in a 3-1 defeat to Liverpool at Anfield. He could easily have been beaten to this honour by two days if George Baddeley had not had the bad luck to twist his knee in his 99th consecutive game on Boxing Day at home to Liverpool.

SATURDAY 1st JANUARY 1944

The prolific Freddie Steele, while home on leave from the forces, made a rare appearance up front for Stoke City and scored six in a 9-3 rout of Wolves in a League Cup qualifying match at the Victoria Ground. Steele only managed to appear in nine games in the 1943/44 season but he still finished with a tally of 20 goals to his name.

FRIDAY 1st JANUARY 1965

The Queen's New Year Honours List revealed that Stanley Matthews was to become the first footballer to be knighted. The Hanley-born winger was still playing top-flight football for Stoke at the time.

SATURDAY 2nd JANUARY 1954

The Second Division match at Upton Park was abandoned with West Ham United leading 4-1. The match, which was abandoned with only six minutes remaining on the clock, was replayed in April with Stoke earning a point thanks to a brace from Neville 'Tim' Coleman.

SATURDAY 2nd JANUARY 1971

Stoke beat Millwall 2-1 at the Victoria Ground thanks to John Ritchie and Jimmy Greenhoff. Victory came after Millwall had taken a first-minute lead. The FA Cup third round clash was the start of a Cup adventure that would end with Stoke appearing in two consecutive semi-finals, both of which would end in replays against Arsenal.

SATURDAY 3rd JANUARY 1942

A rare double hat-trick was scored by Stoke's Tommy Sale in the 8-0 wartime League Cup qualifying victory against Staffordshire rivals Walsall. The win came in front of 3,000 fans at the Victoria Ground.

SATURDAY 3RD JANUARY 1976

Force 11 winds overnight caused havoc throughout the area and nowhere more so than at the Victoria Ground where a large section of the Butler Street stand roof was blown off. This turned out to be a bigger blow to the club than first appeared as the team was broken up in order to pay for repairs. It was not bad news for everybody at the club. Full-back Mike Pejic took advantage by collecting the wood which had been blown off to use as firewood!

SATURDAY 4TH JANUARY 1890

Harry Simpson failed to turn up for the league match at Blackburn Rovers and Stoke had to play the game with only ten men. Rovers took full advantage of the situation and scored eight without reply.

SATURDAY 4TH JANUARY 1902

A number of Stoke players fell violently ill after eating fish for lunch at a local café before the game at Liverpool. The well-known amateur Dr Leigh Richmond Roose could do little to prevent the 7-0 defeat, either as a goalkeeper or as a physician. It was so bad that the Potters started the second-half with only seven players on the pitch!

SATURDAY 4TH JANUARY 1913

Northampton Town demolished Stoke 9-0 in a Southern League Division One match, watched by a small crowd of just 1,600.

SATURDAY 4TH JANUARY 1964

Stoke set off on an FA Cup run which went as far as the fifth round by beating Portsmouth 4-1 at the Victoria Ground. The goals were shared between Dennis Viollet and John Ritchie.

SATURDAY 5TH JANUARY 1918

Oldham Athletic visited Stoke in the War League and lost 7-0 in front of 5,000 fans. Billy Herbert grabbed four, Howell scored two and James Martin got one. Martin was a £750 buy from Stoke St Peter's. He played half of his 32 games for Stoke in wartime and joined Aberdare Athletic in 1921.

SATURDAY 5TH JANUARY 1946

In the 1946/47 season – the first post-war – each round of the FA Cup was played over two legs. Stoke kicked off with a 3-1 home win over Burnley, and then progressed to the fourth round 4-3 on aggregate despite a 2-1 defeat in the return leg at Turf Moor two days later.

WEDNESDAY 5TH JANUARY 1972

Hillsborough was selected as the venue for the League Cup semi-final replay against West Ham United. Stoke had the best of the game but could not force a goal, even after 30 minutes extra time. The venue of the second replay in the epic tie, Old Trafford, was in Stoke's favour.

SATURDAY 5TH JANUARY 2002

David Moyes' Everton side visited the Britannia Stadium in the third round of the FA Cup to face Gudjon Thordarson's Stoke. City played defensively and there were few chances in a game most noted for the midfield duel between Karl Henry and Everton's Paul Gascoigne. The Toffees eventually prevailed thanks to an Alan Stubbs free-kick.

SATURDAY 6TH JANUARY 1917

The first game played by Stoke in 1917 ended with a convincing 7-0 defeat of Bolton Wanderers. Whittingham, Howell, and Herbert each scored a brace and Charlie Parker got the other in a 7-0 victory.

SATURDAY 6TH JANUARY 1979

The third round FA Cup tie against Oldham Athletic had to be abandoned in the second half due to fog. Stoke were leading 2-0 at the Victoria Ground

SATURDAY 6TH JANUARY 1996

Premiership Nottingham Forest forced a replay against the Potters in the FA Cup third round. Stoke were easily the better team and took the lead through Simon Sturridge, before hitting the post, having shots cleared off the line, and Lee Sandford hitting his own player with Crossley beaten. Late on Forest striker Jason Lee miskicked badly, the ball fortuitously fell to Stuart Pearce and he buried it. Forest won the replay 2-0 at the City Ground.

SUNDAY 6TH JANUARY 2008

Live on BBC1 for the first time, Stoke nearly produced a cup shock against Premiership Newcastle United. Ryan Shawcross and Leon Cort kept Toon strikers Michael Owen and Mark Viduka at bay. The best chances fell to City as both Ricardo Fuller and Jon Parkin went close, but the match finished goalless. Newcastle won the replay 4-1, Liam Lawrence scoring Stoke's goal.

MONDAY 7TH JANUARY 1888

Stoke reached the fifth round of the FA Cup for the first time in their history, but were defeated 4-1 at West Bromwich Albion. Progress to this stage was helped by a bye in the fourth round.

SATURDAY 7TH JANUARY 1893

The joint lowest home gate ever – recorded as 1,000 – turned up to see Stoke thrash Newton Heath, who later became Manchester United, by a 7-1 scoreline. Billy Dickson scored a hat-trick and the Fife-born centre-forward finished with a career tally of 48 goals in 134 games for Stoke. He won one cap for Scotland, scoring four in a 10-2 victory over Ireland.

SATURDAY 7TH JANUARY 1922

The FA Cup first round draw threw up a local derby at Port Vale. Arty Watkin scored a hat-trick as Stoke moved into the next round in front of 14,471 at the Old Recreation Ground in Hanley. Arty Watkin scored 77 goals in 177 games for Stoke either side of the First World War, until his retirement in 1927.

SATURDAY 7TH JANUARY 1978

The FA Cup draw was kind to Stoke as it paired them with Tilbury, of the Isthmian League Premier Division, in the third round. City went 3-0 up inside half an hour – thanks to Jeff Cook, David Gregory and Steve Waddington – and then added a fourth through Cook. The game signalled the end of George Eastham's short stint as manager as he resigned soon afterwards, having won just nine of his 37 league matches in charge.

SATURDAY 8th JANUARY 1910

Having already beaten Burton United 7-1 and 5-0 in the Southern League, Stoke hosted them again in the Birmingham League and again scored heavily, this time winning 8-0. Amos Baddeley grabbed his second hat-trick of the three matches as Stoke cruised to victory.

SATURDAY 8th JANUARY 1944

Just seven days after beating Wolverhampton Wanderers 9-3 at the Victoria Ground in the Football League Cup, Stoke were at it again beating Aston Villa 6-3. Freddie Steele, who had scored six against Wolves, had returned to the forces and his place was taken by Syd Peppitt. The reserve forward scored a hat-trick, as did Tommy Sale, to ensure victory in front of a decent wartime crowd of 16,492.

MONDAY 8th JANUARY 1951

Stoke City defeated local rivals Port Vale in an FA Cup third round replay at the Valiants' new home, Vale Park. After a 2-2 draw in the first match, Frank Bowyer scored the only goal of a tight game in front of over 40,000 fans to dump Vale out of the cup.

SATURDAY 9th JANUARY 1954

Frank Bowyer notched four in the FA Cup third round against Hartlepools United as Stoke won 6-2. The Potters lost 3-1 after a replay to Leicester City in the next round, Malkin grabbing the goal.

TUESDAY 9th JANUARY 1979

Luther Blissett struck twice in extra time to send Watford into the League Cup semi-final at Stoke's expense. The Potters missed a great chance to progress against Graham Taylor's Third Division side.

SUNDAY 9th JANUARY 2005

Wayne Thomas scored just before half-time to give Stoke the lead at Highbury and send the travelling army of Stokies into delirium. Arsenal came back in the second half to win this FA Cup third round match with goals from Reyes and Van Persie. It could have been different as Ade Akinbiyi hit the bar and also had a goal disallowed.

SATURDAY 10TH JANUARY 1959

Stoke-born former Wolves forward Dennis Wilshaw scored a hat-trick as City beat Oldham 5-1 in the FA Cup third round. Stoke initially missed out on local lad Wilshaw who went to Wolverhampton Wanderers instead and forged a fine career scoring 117 in 232 games whilst at Molineux. He won 12 caps for England and eventually moved to Stoke in 1957, scoring 50 goals in 108 appearances for the Potters before retiring in 1961 through injury.

WEDNESDAY 10TH JANUARY 1998

The worst home league defeat in the club's history came just days after several players heard, through the local media, that they were no longer required by the club. With team morale obviously at a low ebb, Birmingham City eased to a 7-0 victory. The humiliation prompted some home fans to attempt to climb into the directors' box in order to vent their anger.

SATURDAY 11TH JANUARY 1908

The first round of the FA Cup paired Stoke with Lincoln and the Potters ran out comfortable 5-0 winners at the Victoria Ground. Two of Stoke's goals were scored by George Gallimore. Gallimore was an unpredictable forward who scored 17 goals for Stoke before moving to Sheffield United when the club went bust at the end of the season.

SATURDAY 11TH JANUARY 1930

The FA Cup third round tie at Doncaster Rovers was abandoned after 76 minutes with Stoke leading 3-2. The game was replayed at Belle Vue just five days later with Rovers prevailing 1-0.

WEDNESDAY 12TH JANUARY 1955

After a 1-1 draw at Gigg Lane, Bury arrived at the Victoria Ground for an FA Cup third round replay. Don Ratcliffe scored for City but the game finished level after 90 minutes and went into extra time. The additional period was eventually abandoned after 112 minutes with the scores still level at 1-1. The game would go on to become Stoke's longest ever cup tie.

TUESDAY 12TH JANUARY 1988

Despite Scott Barrett producing a wonderful display of goalkeeping at Anfield in the FA Cup replay, Liverpool progressed to the fourth round thanks to Peter Beardsley's mis-hit shot early in the match. The replay came after a goalless draw which should have been won by Graham Shaw who hesitated when clean through. Mick Mills said of Shaw that he believed he was a better prospect than David Platt – then at Crewe Alexandra – and that is why he did not sign the future England midfielder!

SATURDAY 13TH JANUARY 1923

A visit to North Eastern League side Blyth Spartans was the prize for Stoke in the first round of the FA Cup. Blyth did not prove to be too much of an obstacle – this time – and 9,121 witnessed an easy 3-0 victory for the visitors thanks to two goals for Jimmy Broad and one for Dai Nicholas. Stoke lost 3-1 to Bury in the next round, with Broad notching yet another cup goal.

MONDAY 13TH JANUARY 1958

Stoke finally beat Aston Villa in an FA Cup second replay at neutral Molineux. After drawing 1-1 and 3-3, Stoke came out on top 2-0 thanks to Tim Coleman and Bobby Cairns strikes.

SATURDAY 13TH JANUARY 1996

Simon Sturridge netted the only goal of the game to give Stoke victory over Leicester City at the Victoria Ground to move them above the visitors to fourth in the table. The Foxes would later be Stoke's play-off opponents.

SATURDAY 13TH JANUARY 1998

Stoke lost to West Bromwich Albion for the first time in a decade in the FA Cup third round tie at the Hawthorns. Marco Gabbiadini notched the only Stoke goal as the Baggies ran out 3-1 winners. Stoke's overall record against West Brom in the league is fantastic having won 52 compared to the Baggies' 38. However, Stoke have yet to win in the FA Cup in five attempts.

SATURDAY 14TH JANUARY 1928

Gillingham visited the Potteries in the FA Cup third round and a small crowd of 5,234 witnessed Stoke cruise through – to a tie against Bolton Wanderers in the next round – with a 6-1 win. Charlie Wilson grabbed two of the goals and there was one each for Tom Williamson, Bobby Archibald, Walter Bussey and Harry Davies.

SATURDAY 14TH JANUARY 1939

Stoke's rise up the First Division table continued with a 6-3 victory over Birmingham City at the Victoria Ground. The win was largely down to Freddie Steele who scored four goals for the third time in his Stoke career. Overall, he would achieve this feat six times for the Potters, and no other striker can come near to this record.

MONDAY 14TH JANUARY 2008

Stoke City broke their transfer record by signing Leon Cort from Crystal Palace for £1.2m after he had spent a successful two-month loan period at the Britannia Stadium. Cort's headed goals from corners and long throws – which totalled 8 from 35 games during the season – helped Stoke to promotion to the Premiership in 2007/08. The former Southend United and Hull City defender developed a solid partnership at the back with young Ryan Shawcross.

SATURDAY 15TH JANUARY 1927

Stoke's promotion rivals, Bradford Park Avenue, beat the Potters 3-0 in front of an impressive crowd of 21,458 at their Park Avenue ground. The Yorkshire side reduced the gap at the top of Division Three North to just five points although Nelson, who were level on points with Bradford, had three games in hand.

WEDNESDAY 15TH JANUARY 1936

Freddie Steele scored a hat-trick in the 4-0 FA Cup fourth round victory against Millwall at the Victoria Ground. Steele scored a total of 24 hat-tricks for the club, including 10 in wartime football, with only strike partner Tommy Sale scoring more. Included in this total are two fives and one double hat-trick.

MONDAY 15TH JANUARY 1962

FA Cup holders Leicester City had the defence of their crown emphatically halted by the Potters in a third round replay. Having drawn 1-1 at Filbert Street thanks to a Jackie Mudie goal, Stoke turned on the style to win 5-2 with the goals coming from Tony Allen, Peter Bullock, Stanley Matthews, John Nibloe and Tommy Thompson. Amongst the 38,525 onlookers was Dennis Viollet who had signed earlier in the day for a fee of £22,000 from Manchester United.

SATURDAY 15TH JANUARY 1972

Third Division Chesterfield almost forced the FA Cup third round tie into a replay, but Stoke hung on. The win set them en route to the semi-final, with Terry Conroy and Peter Dobing scoring. Dubliner Conroy played in over 300 games for Stoke despite many injuries.

TUESDAY 16TH JANUARY 1926

Dick Johnson scored four times in the 5-0 victory at home to Fulham. Johnson had signed for Stoke from Liverpool in 1925 for £1,200 and over the next four and a half years he scored 25 goals in 83 first-team games before leaving for New Brighton in September 1929, and then on to Connah's Quay.

SATURDAY 16TH JANUARY 1937

Birmingham City were knocked out of the FA Cup at the Victoria ground in front of 31,480. Freddie Steele notched a hat-trick and Joe Johnson grabbed the other in the 4-1 win. Preston North End beat Stoke 5-1 in the next round.

FRIDAY 16TH JANUARY 1998

Keith Humphreys had taken over from Peter Coates as chairman in the run up to the match and several thousand City fans registered their displeasure at the state of the club by turning up 15 minutes late for the game. Stoke came from behind to register a rare win thanks to Richard Forsyth's penalty and a Peter Thorne shot. Despite the win, Chic Bates was still sacked due to his overall record which stood at just eight wins in 27 matches.

SATURDAY 17TH JANUARY 1891

In the first round of the FA Cup Stoke were drawn at home to the only Football League champions so far, Preston North End. Stoke managed to pull off a wonderful 3-0 victory after goals from Louis Ballham, Peter Coupar and Peter Turner. Coupar had come down to Stoke from Dundee but never settled in the area and returned to Dundee after only five months.

SATURDAY 17TH JANUARY 1976

With the Victoria Ground out of action after the roof had blown off the Butler Street Stand, Stoke hired Vale Park from their local rivals for the First Division match against Middlesbrough. At half-time Mike Pejic had to go to hospital due to a stomach upset and the game looked to be heading for a draw until Ian Moores latched on to a poor back-pass to grab the winner. The Potters moved up to seventh in front of 21,009 in what was the only top-flight match to be played in Burslem.

WEDNESDAY 17TH JANUARY 1979

Oldham Athletic won the replay of an abandoned cup tie 1-0 at the Victoria Ground: Stoke were winning the first attempt 2-0 at the time of abandonment. Of the three FA Cup ties abandoned whilst Stoke were leading, none have been won once replayed.

TUESDAY 17TH JANUARY 2006

Staffordshire rivals Tamworth of the Nationwide Conference nearly caused an upset in the FA Cup third round replay. Paul Gallagher saved City's blushes by equalising in the 80th minute at The Lamb to take the tie into extra time. Stoke eventually won on penalties, only the second success in 12 penalty shoot-outs.

SATURDAY 18TH JANUARY 1890

The Old Westminsters visited Stoke in the FA Cup for a game watched by a crowd of 3,000. Stoke won the tie comfortably 3-0 and went on to face Everton in the second round, thanks to goals from Freddie Gee, Jimmy Sayer and Bob Ramsay.

FRIDAY 18TH JANUARY 2008

Young defender Ryan Shawcross made his move from Manchester United to Stoke City permanent after spending the first half of the season on loan. The fee was initially £1m, possibly rising to £2m, depending on appearances and club success. The tall and strong England under-21 international achieved promotion to the Premiership with Stoke City in his first season of senior football.

MONDAY 19TH JANUARY 1931

Manchester United finally defeated Stoke at the third time of asking in the FA Cup third round. Tom Mather's side were beaten 4-2 at neutral Anfield in the second replay, despite goals from Bobby Archibald and Bobby Liddle, after the first two games had finished 3-3 and 0-0.

TUESDAY 19TH JANUARY 1988

The third round of the Simod Cup saw Stoke travel to Leicester City and, after a 0-0 draw, the Potters won their first ever penalty shoot-out at the fifth attempt. Being drawn away in every round of the competition finally caught up with Stoke at Luton Town in the quarter-final, as they crashed out 4-1.

THURSDAY 19TH JANUARY 2006

Reading signed defender John Halls from Stoke for £250,000. Halls played the majority of his 74 games for the club at right-back after signing from Arsenal for the same fee two years earlier after a successful loan spell with the Potters.

SATURDAY 20TH JANUARY 1940

Stoke travelled to Old Trafford in the War League and lost 4-3 to Manchester United. Stoke's scorers were Syd Peppitt, Tommy Sale and Frank Bowyer, who made his debut in this game although it would be six years before his official first team debut, nine years after signing professional forms, and at the age of 25. Bowyer still reached 435 appearances – excluding wartime games – for the club, and his goalscoring record of 137 league goals is second only to Steele. He has also notched 12 in the FA Cup and 56 in wartime football.

WEDNESDAY 20TH JANUARY 1993

During the defence of the Autoglass Trophy Stoke took on Barnet at the Victoria Ground in the only competitive game between the two clubs and won 4-1 thanks to a hat-trick from Steve Foley. After beating West Bromwich Albion in the next round, Stoke went out 1-0 to the eventual winners Port Vale in the quarter-final, despite being dominant throughout the match.

SATURDAY 21ST JANUARY 1989

There was a great deal of media attention on Ipswich Town's new Russian import Sergei Baltacha before the Second Division clash with Stoke at Portman Road. Baltacha scored in the 5-1 win for Town yet Mick Mills claimed that Stoke were the better side between Ipswich's goals!

SATURDAY 21ST JANUARY 2006

Johan Boskamp's Stoke tried to play attacking football and this meant that there were times when the team found themselves on the end of a beating. Hull City visited the 'Brit' for a Championship clash and went away with a 3-0 win. The Tigers took the points after a Darel Russell own goal and one each for future Stoke striker Jon Parkin and Darryl Duffy. The Hull side also included ex-Potter Keith Andrews and future Potter Leon Cort. There were five occasions during the 2006/07 season when City conceded three goals at home, and they lost on each occasion.

WEDNESDAY 22ND JANUARY 1913

Reading hosted Stoke in the FA Cup third round replay and won 3-0 after the first game had ended 2-2. The original tie at the Victoria Ground had been abandoned with Stoke leading 2-1 after 25 minutes.

MONDAY 22ND JANUARY 1923

Stoke beat Blackburn Rovers 5-1 in the replay of a match that was originally abandoned after 86 minutes with Rovers leading 1-0. Jimmy Broad hit a hat-trick in the game to take his tally for the season to 19, on his way to an eventual total of 26.

SATURDAY 22ND JANUARY 1966

Third Division Walsall created a cup upset as they knocked First Division Stoke out of the FA Cup at the Victoria Ground. Trailing 1-0 in first-half stoppage time, Potters keeper Bobby Irvine kicked Walsall forward Allan Clarke who got up to net the penalty and seal the win. This cost Irvine his place in the team and he never played for the club again.

SATURDAY 23RD JANUARY 1892

The original match against the famous London amateur side Corinthians – or Casuals – in the first round of the FA Cup was declared void after Stoke won 3-0. The Potters won the replayed match by the same score.

SATURDAY 23RD JANUARY 1993

A fantastic away following of 7,500 had a wonderful day at the Hawthorns. Ardiles' Albion played all of the football, but Macari's Stoke took all of the points to stay top. The 2-1 Potters victory, thanks to goals from Nigel Gleghorn and Mark Stein, was seen by a crowd of 29,341 which was a large gate for a third tier fixture.

TUESDAY 24TH JANUARY 1922

Cornelius 'Neil' Franklin was born in Stoke-on-Trent. Franklin rose through the ranks at Stoke to emerge as one of the best centre-halves in the country. A regular for Stoke and England, Franklin was poised to go to the World Cup in Brazil, but instead played in a rebel league in Colombia. The episode ended his career at international level, and for Stoke. For the Potters he played in 186 wartime matches and 162 competitive games, without scoring a goal, before playing for Hull City on his return from South America.

MONDAY 24TH JANUARY 1955

Old Trafford was the venue for the fourth replay in the epic third round FA Cup tie versus Bury. In extra time, 'Tim' Coleman scored to send Stoke through 3-2 to meet Swansea Town. The tie had lasted for 9 hours and 22 minutes.

WEDNESDAY 25th JANUARY 1950

Mike Pejic was born in Chesterton, Newcastle-under-Lyme. The combative full-back won four England caps in his career which also included a League Cup winners' medal with the Potters in 1972. Pejic played in 336 games for Stoke before moving on to Everton and then Aston Villa. After he was forced to retire from football through injury in 1980, Pejic dabbled with farming before moving into coaching at a number of clubs including spells at both Stoke City and Port Vale.

TUESDAY 25th JANUARY 2000

A wintry night in Blackpool was the backdrop for a 2-1 Auto Windscreens Shield third round victory. A goal each from Graham Kavanagh and Brynjar Gunnarsson sealed a place in the quarter-finals for Gudjon Thordarson's side. Chesterfield would be the next opponents as Stoke marched on towards a Wembley final.

SATURDAY 26th JANUARY 1907

A 2-0 defeat against Sheffield United at Bramall Lane sent Stoke to the bottom of the First Division. This was a position they would occupy for the rest of the season before being relegated to the Second Division for the very first time along with Derby County.

SATURDAY 26th JANUARY 1924

Stoke visited Clapton Orient in the Second Division and won by two goals to nil. The scorers were Jimmy Broad and Harry Sellars on his debut. The victory sent Stoke back to the top of the Second Division table as they made a bid to bounce straight back into the First Division at the first attempt. They would fall away in the latter part of the season and eventually finished sixth.

SATURDAY 26th JANUARY 1962

Having beaten Leicester City in the third round, Blackburn Rovers were the visitors for Stoke's first ever all-ticket match. The crowd was limited to 50,000 and the FA Cup fourth round tie was actually watched by 49,486. Blackburn won the game 1-0, thanks to a disputed Bryan Douglas penalty.

WEDNESDAY 26TH JANUARY 1972

Stoke finally made it through to their first Wembley final after a League Cup semi-final second replay packed with incident at Old Trafford. Whilst West Ham United keeper Bobby Ferguson was having off-field treatment after being kicked in the head by Terry Conroy, Bobby Moore took over in goal. The Hammers skipper then proceeded to save a penalty from Bernard, but could not prevent him from scoring with the rebound. With Ferguson now back in goal, West Ham went ahead through a Smith own goal, and a Trevor Brooking strike, before Peter Dobing and Conroy scored to send the Stoke contingent in the near 50,000 crowd wild as the Potters hung on to win 3-2.

SATURDAY 27TH JANUARY 1934

Frankie Soo, Tommy Sale and Stanley Matthews scored the goals which knocked Blackpool out of the FA Cup at the fourth round stage in front of 30,091 at the Victoria Ground. The victory set up a fifth round tie against Chelsea. The same scorers and the same result had also knocked out Bradford Park Avenue in the previous round.

SUNDAY 27TH JANUARY 1974

The first ever Sunday First Division game took place between Stoke City and Chelsea, with supporters required to buy a team sheet instead of paying for entry to get round the Sunday trading laws. Nearly 32,000 supporters took advantage to see Stoke win thanks to a Geoff Hurst penalty after Alan Hudson had been fouled by his former team-mate Gary Locke.

SATURDAY 28TH JANUARY 1928

Stoke's FA Cup run continued with a 4-2 victory over Bolton Wanderers in the fourth round. Charlie Wilson scored two for a second consecutive tie to set up a fifth round clash against Manchester City at Maine Road.

TUESDAY 28TH JANUARY 1936

Stoke went to Old Trafford in the FA Cup fourth round replay and proceeded to knock the Red Devils out with goals from Tommy Sale and Billy Robson.

SATURDAY 28TH JANUARY 1984

The lift given to both the team and the crowd by the return of Alan Hudson was obvious as he inspired Stoke to a 1-0 victory over Arsenal. Survival was still remote but became a definite possibility with Paul Maguire's winning goal.

WEDNESDAY 28TH JANUARY 1987

After two tight matches in the third round of the FA Cup, Stoke won the toss to host the second replay at the Victoria Ground against Grimsby Town. The Potters then put in an excellent first-half display to see them go in four ahead at the interval thanks to goals from Brian Talbot, Phil Heath, Nicky Morgan and Carl Saunders. Saunders and Morgan both scored a second goal after the break to complete the 6-0 scoreline and send Stoke through to play Fourth Division Cardiff City in the next round, again at home.

WEDNESDAY 28TH JANUARY 1998

Former Stoke midfielder Chris Kamara took charge of his first game as manager of the club at the County Ground against Swindon Town. With promising young full-back Andy Griffin sold to Newcastle, Kamara's team were beaten by the only goal from Robinson, and the worrying slide down the table continued.

SATURDAY 29TH JANUARY 1927

Having already been defeated by promotion rivals Bradford Park Avenue two weeks earlier, Stoke now succumbed to another of their rivals Nelson, losing by the only goal of the game. The Potters were now only three points clear of Rochdale at the top of Division Three North and just five points away from Nelson who had three games in hand.

TUESDAY 29TH JANUARY 2002

Youth team product Marc Goodfellow scored an injury-time winner against Peterborough United at London Road. The victory lifted Stoke to second place in the Second Division table. Goodfellow never fulfilled his promise and after nine goals in 71 appearances he moved to Bristol City and eventually into non-league with Burton Albion.

SATURDAY 30TH JANUARY 1926

Having knocked Wigan Borough out of the FA Cup in round three, Stoke travelled to Swansea Town for the fourth round tie played in front of a 21,000 crowd. The game produced City's heaviest ever defeat in the FA Cup as they lost 6-3, with the consolation goals coming from Ewart Beswick, Harry Davies and Joe Johnson.

SATURDAY 30TH JANUARY 1982

The visit to the City Ground to take on Brian Clough's Nottingham Forest resulted in a good point for Stoke. Richie Barker had a superb display from Peter Fox to thank as he kept a clean sheet from million pound strikers Justin Fashanu and Ian Wallace.

SATURDAY 31ST JANUARY 1891

Having beaten Preston in the first round of the FA Cup, Stoke were again drawn at home to top opposition, with Aston Villa the visitors. The result was the same though as Stoke again pulled off a 3-0 victory, in front of around 7,000 fans.

TUESDAY 31ST JANUARY 1933

Just 3,908 supporters turned out at Oldham Athletic to see Stoke win 4-0 and return to the top of the Second Division table. The goals came from Joe Johnson with two, Harry Ware and Henry Salmon.

TUESDAY 31ST JANUARY 1995

The curse of penalty shoot-outs struck again as Stoke lost to Notts County in the Anglo-Italian Cup semi-final, both legs having finished 0-0. County went on to win the final beating Ascoli 2-1 at Wembley Stadium.

SATURDAY 1st FEBRUARY 1896

Willie Maxwell scored a hat-trick for Stoke and Allan Maxwell and Billy Dickson grabbed the other two as they eased past Tottenham Hotspur 5-0 in the FA Cup first round at the 'Vic'. The victory earned them a trip to Turf Moor, the home of Burnley, in the second round.

SATURDAY 1st FEBRUARY 1930

Stoke visited Ashton Gate for the Second Division match with Bristol City, played in front of just over 10,000 fans. Tom Mather's Potters ran out 6-2 winners thanks to goals from Wilf Kirkham, Walter Bussey and four, including a penalty, from Charlie Wilson.

MONDAY 1st FEBRUARY 1932

For the second successive year a neutral venue was required to separate Stoke City and their opponents in the FA Cup. On this occasion Sunderland met Stoke at Maine Road in the fourth round. Unlike the previous year's tie against Manchester United, City came out on top thanks to a Joe Mawson brace after extra time. The cup run would come to an end against Bury at Gigg Lane in the fifth round.

SATURDAY 2nd FEBRUARY 1895

Newton Heath played host to Stoke in the FA Cup first round at their Bank Street ground. A goal from Jimmie Robertson and two from Sammy Meston ensured it was Stoke into the second round of the competition. The Potters went on to lose 2-0 away at Sheffield Wednesday.

SATURDAY 3rd FEBRUARY 1945

The wartime international between England and Scotland at Villa Park saw Stoke players Frank Soo, Neil Franklin and Stanley Matthews all representing England. This was a regular sight as all three Stoke players appeared in a number of wartime internationals.

WEDNESDAY 3rd FEBRUARY 1892

For the third year in a row Stoke had reached the FA Cup quarter-final stage. This time they hosted Sunderland and managed to force a replay as the match ended 2-2 with goals from Turner and Schofield.

SATURDAY 3RD FEBRUARY 1917

Bob Whittingham netted four goals in the 6-0 wartime victory over Burnley, with Billy Herbert and guest player Harrison getting the others. Guest players were a regular feature of football during both wartime periods as players appeared for other clubs.

SATURDAY 3RD FEBRUARY 1945

A 1-0 defeat at Maine Road was not enough to prevent Stoke City from reaching the wartime League Cup Final for the first time in their history. The Potters progressed 2-1 on aggregate to face Leicester City in the final, which was then played over two legs. Bill Asprey and John Ritchie had scored the vital goals in the first leg 18 days earlier at the Victoria Ground

SATURDAY 4TH FEBRUARY 1911

Stoke visited Chesham Town in the Southern League and had a field day. Both Billy Smith and Ernie Boulton scored hat-tricks in the 8-0 success. This was one of three times Stoke scored eight or more in the 1910/11 season as they scored a total of 175 goals in all competition.

THURSDAY 4TH FEBRUARY 1937

A disappointing gate of just 8,224 – the lowest gate of the season – saw Stoke thrash West Bromwich Albion 10-3 at the Victoria Ground and achieve their record league victory. The win was largely thanks to the prolific Freddie Steele who scored five of the goals. The scoring was completed by two goals each for Joe Johnson and George Antonio and also a penalty from Arthur Turner.

SATURDAY 5TH FEBRUARY 1927

A hard fought 3-2 success at home to Chesterfield restored Stoke's five point lead at the top of Division Three North after two defeats in the previous three games to their promotion rivals.

SATURDAY 5TH FEBRUARY 1972

Stoke visited Tranmere Rovers in the fourth round of the FA Cup and earned a replay thanks to goals from Terry Conroy and John Ritchie. The attendance of 24,426 was a record crowd for a game at Prenton Park.

THURSDAY 6TH FEBRUARY 1958

The Munich air disaster took the life of Harry Davies, a journalist and former footballer. Davies was an amateur England international who played just one Southern League game for Stoke in 1913.

MONDAY 6TH FEBRUARY 1961

After two goalless ties, the fourth round FA Cup tie against Aldershot was settled at the neutral venue of Molineux with Dennis Wilshaw scoring twice in a 3-0 win at his former stamping ground. The victory set up a tie at Newcastle United.

SATURDAY 6TH FEBRUARY 1965

Sir Stanley Matthews set the record as the oldest Football League player. The 3-1 victory over Fulham, thanks to two goals from Dennis Viollet and one from John Ritchie, saw Stan applauded off the field aged 50 years and five days after his only appearance of the season. Matthews, voted as Footballer of the Year in 1963, finished with a Stoke City total of 355 senior appearances, and 62 goals.

MONDAY 6TH FEBRUARY 1978

Alan A'Court's second and final game in charge as caretaker manager was against Northern Premier League side Blyth Spartans in the FA Cup fourth round. The pitch was a mess but Stoke managed to lead 2-1 with only 15 minutes left before Blyth came back to win it with Terry Johnson's 88th minute strike. The 18,765 present applauded as the minnows went on a lap of honour.

WEDNESDAY 7TH FEBRUARY 1962

Stoke City and Wigan Athletic accounted for the entire professional career of John Butler, who was born on this day in Liverpool. Butler, who joined Wigan Athletic from Prescott Cables, moved to Stoke in December 1988 for £75,000 and quickly established himself as a first-team regular. Mick Mills' eye for a full-back had again picked up a gem after his first full-back signing Lee Dixon had been sold on to Arsenal. Butler made 319 senior appearances for the Potters, before transferring back to Wigan in 1995.

SATURDAY 7th FEBRUARY 1987

Stoke extended their unbeaten run to 11 league games with a 3-1 win at home to Crystal Palace. A crowd of just over 13,000 were there to see Stoke reach fourth place in the Second Division table thanks to strikes from Tony Ford, Lee Dixon and George Berry.

WEDNESDAY 8th FEBRUARY 1922

Stoke visited Gigg Lane and came away with a 1-0 victory over Bury in front of 7,000 spectators. The win put Stoke into the promotion places for the first time in the 1921/22 season and – with the exception of just seven days – they would stay in the top two throughout.

TUESDAY 8th FEBRUARY 1938

Possibly the most famous newspaper headline in the club's history hit the streets as the *Evening Sentinel* announced 'Stanley Matthews' Bombshell for Stoke City'. Ongoing friction between club, manager and player had led to Stan requesting a transfer and supporters were in uproar at the possibility of losing their hero. As interested clubs started to circle the England winger, an uneasy truce was reached, and Matthews would remain at the club for another nine years.

MONDAY 8th FEBRUARY 1971

Old Trafford was the neutral venue selected for the second replay of the FA Cup fourth round tie with Huddersfield Town. Stoke overcame an injury crisis to win 1-0 with Jimmy Greenhoff scoring the winner.

SATURDAY 8th FEBRUARY 1975

Tony Waddington's side recorded the only ever league win by a Stoke team at White Hart Lane thanks to first-half goals from Jimmy Greenhoff and Alan Hudson, as Tottenham Hotspur were beaten 2-0.

SATURDAY 9th FEBRUARY 1935

Bob McGrory's Stoke side beat Blackburn Rovers 3-1 at the Victoria Ground to move up to fourth place in the First Division. Any hopes of a first Football League title slipped away as only three of the last 14 matches were won and they ended the season in tenth place.

WEDNESDAY 9TH FEBRUARY 1972

Stoke City prevailed 2-0 in the FA Cup fourth round replay against ten-man Tranmere Rovers after Yeats was sent off for punching Mike Bernard, the goals coming from Bernard and Jimmy Greenhoff. The replay was only necessary after Stoke surrendered a two-goal lead in the last ten minutes at Prenton Park.

SATURDAY 9TH FEBRUARY 2008

A thrilling match at Molineux saw Stoke take all three points, winning 4-2. Coming back from 2-1 down, controversy surrounded the victory. With Stoke leading 3-2 and with time running out, Wolves appealed for a penalty which was turned down. Whilst the players were still appealing, Stoke broke to the other end and scored their fourth through substitute Ricardo Fuller, who was on the bench after returning from international duty with Jamaica. The other Stoke goals were claimed by Leon Cort, Liam Lawrence and Rory Delap.

MONDAY 10TH FEBRUARY 1908

It took a second replay on a neutral ground at Nottingham in front of 5,000 before the FA Cup second round tie against Gainsborough Trinity was settled. Goals from Mart Watkins, Tom Holford and Freddie Brown sent Stoke to a 3-2 victory, and on to Portsmouth for the next round, after the first two ties had finished 1-1 and 2-2, respectively.

SATURDAY 10TH FEBRUARY 1945

Stanley Matthews played a large part in the 7-0 victory over Chester City in the wartime League Cup. Stan tormented the visiting defence as Tommy Sale and Alf Basnett both grabbed hat-tricks with Frank Mountford netting the other in front of 12,000 fans. Stoke had won 3-2 in the first fixture against Chester just seven days earlier.

SATURDAY 11TH FEBRUARY 1922

The visit to Filbert Street to take on Leicester City in the Second Division saw Stoke eventually prevail 4-3 in a fantastic match. The bumper crowd of 21,000 saw Stoke triumph as Fred Groves bagged two and Jimmy Broad and Billy Tempest scored one each.

SATURDAY 11TH FEBRUARY 1933

Stoke's promotion prospects looked good after the 2-1 win at Burnley moved them back into the top two with Joe Mawson and Harry Sellars scoring.

SATURDAY 12TH FEBRUARY 1966

Struggling Northampton Town visited the Victoria Ground for the First Division fixture in front of 16,525 fans. Stoke showed no mercy against the Cobblers as they won 6-2 with John Ritchie netting four and the others going to Roy Vernon and Peter Dobing.

WEDNESDAY 12TH FEBRUARY 1992

Mark Stein scored the only goal of the game to defeat West Bromwich Albion and send Stoke to the top of the Third Division. A season's best crowd of 23,645 were there to see City knock the Baggies off top spot in the top-of-the-table clash.

TUESDAY 12TH FEBRUARY 2008

It was a real game of two halves at the Britannia Stadium as Stoke raced into a 3-0 half-time lead thanks to Ryan Shawcross, Mama Sidibe and an own goal from Darren Powell. After the break Southampton came back with Stern John scoring two in eight minutes, and despite a tense finish, Stoke held on and took all three points to move third.

SATURDAY 13TH FEBRUARY 1926

The relegation season of 1925/26 saw the emergence of a Potters pre-war stalwart, Billy Spencer. He made his debut in the 2-1 victory at home to Portsmouth and did not miss another game all season as Stoke fought a losing battle against the drop to Division Three.

SATURDAY 13TH FEBRUARY 1932

Bury were 3-0 victors in the FA Cup fifth round clash at Gigg Lane. Stoke had reached this stage largely due to Joe Mawson's four goals in the competition. Mawson left the mines to sign professional forms with Stoke in 1929 and scored on his league debut at Swansea. He was leading scorer in both 1931/32 and 1932/33 before transferring to Nottingham Forest. His Stoke record was 50 goals in 93 appearances.

SATURDAY 14TH FEBRUARY 1891

In the quarter-final of the FA Cup for the second year in a row, Stoke again came unstuck, this time away to Notts County. Only one goal separated the sides in front of around 16,000 supporters.

SATURDAY 14TH FEBRUARY 1987

Stoke's 11-game unbeaten run came to a juddering halt at the Hawthorns as West Bromwich Albion claimed a 4-1 victory. Former Potters striker Garth Crooks grabbed a brace as Phil Heath was sent off for Stoke. Keith Bertschin scored the Potters' consolation goal. The game saw Hans Segers play his only game in goal for Stoke.

SATURDAY 15TH FEBRUARY 1936

Stoke travelled to Barnsley for an FA Cup fifth round tie witnessed by 40,245, a record for Oakwell. The majority of the crowd went home happy as the Tykes won 2-1. Harry Davies bagged the Stoke goal, making him only the second person to pass 100 goals for the club.

SATURDAY 15TH FEBRUARY 1947

A week after being knocked out of the FA Cup at the fifth round stage by Sheffield United, the Potters played host to Chelsea in a First Division game as they moved closer to a possible first-ever league title. A crowd of 30,469 turned out to see an emphatic victory at the Victoria Ground. Syd Peppit and Alec Ormston each bagged a brace in the 6-1 win, with the scoring being completed by Johnny Sellars and Frank Baker.

WEDNESDAY 15TH FEBRUARY 1956

Stoke travelled to St James' Park for an FA Cup fifth round tie in front of 61,540. Johnny King scored for Stoke but it was not enough as Newcastle United won 2-1. King was a steady goalscorer for Stoke after signing from Crewe for £8,000 and going on to score 113 goals in 371 appearances. He also came close to qualifying for the Wimbledon Championships as a doubles tennis player with fellow Stoke forward George Kelly.

SATURDAY 15TH FEBRUARY 1975

Stoke scored twice in the last three minutes to earn a point at home to Wolverhampton Wanderers, which was enough to send them to the top of the First Division. It was not all good news for Stoke as Mike Pejic broke his leg and play also had to be stopped twice due to crowd trouble.

FRIDAY 15TH FEBRUARY 2008

Another game of two halves as Stoke City pushed for promotion to the Premiership. The 20,979 fans in the ground were stunned as relegation probables Scunthorpe United raced into a two-goal lead inside 20 minutes, the first coming from ex-Stokie Martin Paterson. Stoke flew at the visitors after the break and three goals in fourteen minutes – two for Liam Lawrence and one for Richard Cresswell – won the match. Stoke were top of the Championship for the first time that season and the Premiership dream started to become a reality.

SATURDAY 16TH FEBRUARY 1952

In the days before substitutes, goalkeeper Dennis Herod hurt his arm at Villa Park and was unable to continue in goal. To avoid playing a man short, he went to play on the wing and was largely left unmarked by the Aston Villa defence. Herod scored the winning goal in a 3-2 victory.

TUESDAY 16TH FEBRUARY 1971

Ipswich Town appeared to have done the hard work in forcing the FA Cup fifth round tie to a replay at Portman Road. In the replay, however, Denis Smith popped up late on in East Anglia to win it for the Potters and set up a quarter-final with Hull City at Boothferry Park.

SUNDAY 16TH FEBRUARY 2003

Claudio Ranieri's Chelsea visited the Britannia Stadium and 26,615 turned out to see the FA Cup fifth round tie. Stoke played well but could not get past Carlo Cudicini in the Blues goal. Second-half goals from Hasselbaink and Gronkjaer settled it in favour of the Premier League side.

SATURDAY 17TH FEBRUARY 1934

A crowd of 42,213 cheered Stoke City into the FA Cup quarter-final with a 3-1 win over Chelsea. Stanley Matthews scored twice and Joe Johnson once to set up a clash with Manchester City at Maine Road.

SATURDAY 17TH FEBRUARY 1945

George Mountford scored five times against Port Vale in a War League Cup game, in which Stoke ran out 8-1 winners. The return game at the Old Recreation Ground in Hanley would also result in a trouncing for Vale, this time by a 6-2 scoreline.

TUESDAY 17TH FEBRUARY 1976

Sunderland and Stoke were heading towards a second replay in the FA Cup fifth round, but the Second Division side won it after three goals in four minutes. The 47,583 at Roker Park saw Sunderland go ahead through Holden on 76 minutes. Denis Smith equalised from the kick-off, before Robson won it for the Black Cats three minutes later.

WEDNESDAY 17TH FEBRUARY 1996

Third place in the First Division was the highest spot Stoke would reach in 1995/96, which was their highest position since top-flight relegation in 1985. This position was reached by beating Birmingham City 1-0 with Simon Sturridge scoring against his former club.

SATURDAY 18TH FEBRUARY 1961

For the second time in just six years Stoke faced an FA Cup fifth round tie at St James' Park, and for the second time Newcastle United were victorious with Johnny King again scoring Stoke's consolation. The game also marked Dennis Wilshaw's last game for the club as he was forced to retire at the end of the season through injury.

TUESDAY 18TH FEBRUARY 1964

Stoke lost the FA Cup fifth round replay 2-0 at the Vetch Field – home of Swansea Town – in front of 29,582. In the original tie, which had finished 2-2, Stanley Matthews had scored Stoke's goal, becoming the oldest scorer of an FA Cup goal aged 49 years and 17 days.

SATURDAY 19th FEBRUARY 1944

Without the war Freddie Steele and Tommy Sale would undoubtedly have formed Stoke's most prolific strike partnership. Between them they totalled 522 goals for the Potters although 260 of these came during wartime. In the 8-2 wartime victory at the Hawthorns, Steele scored four and Sale three, with Frank Bowyer netting the other goal.

SATURDAY 19th FEBRUARY 2005

Kenwyne Jones, the Trinidadian on loan from Southampton, netted Stoke's winner against Millwall at the New Den after 15 minutes. City's recent games had not been exciting. This was the 17th consecutive league game with a maximum of only one goal in it. The Stoke fans christened the dull sequence of results as 'binary football'.

SATURDAY 20th FEBRUARY 1892

The FA Cup quarter-final replay saw Sunderland beat Stoke City 4-0 in the north-east after a 2-2 draw at the Victoria Ground in the first match. The Mackems went on to lose their semi-final to Aston Villa.

THURSDAY 20th FEBRUARY 1896

After a 1-1 draw at Turf Moor with Billy Dickson on the score-sheet, Burnley came to the Victoria Ground for the FA Cup second round replay, and were well beaten 7-1. Stoke moved into the quarter-final – the club's fifth – against Wolves thanks to four goals for Tom Hyslop and one each from Billy Dickson, Allan Maxwell and Willie Maxwell.

SATURDAY 20th FEBRUARY 1993

Stoke extended their unbeaten run in the league to 25 games as they beat Bradford City, ironically the last team to beat them, 1-0 thanks to a Dave Kevan strike. The Potters were now ten points clear at the top of the Second Division after the match, seen by a crowd of 16,494.

SATURDAY 20th FEBRUARY 1999

Referee Rob Styles sent off two Millwall players in the match at the New Den, in the third and 70th minutes. The Lions still managed to beat Brian Little's Stoke 2-0, even with only nine men.

SATURDAY 21st FEBRUARY 1976

Tottenham Hotspur took all the points from the Victoria Ground thanks to a 2-1 win, with Jimmy Greenhoff netting Stoke's goal. The game marked the final appearance of Eric Skeels, who had made his debut almost 16 years previously. The industrious Skeels left with the all-time Stoke City appearance record – excluding wartime matches – of 593 games, scoring seven goals in the process.

SATURDAY 21st FEBRUARY 1987

Stoke reached the fifth round of the FA Cup for the first time in 11 years after beating Grimsby Town and Cardiff City in earlier rounds. Coventry City were the visitors as 31,255 – the biggest gate for seven years – packed into the Victoria Ground. Future Stokie Micky Gynn scored the only goal of the game for First Division Coventry, but Stoke had very strong penalty claims turned down when full-back Lee Dixon was felled by Phillips. The Sky Blues went on to win the trophy.

SATURDAY 22nd FEBRUARY 1890

The initial FA Cup quarter-final against Wolves was ordered to be replayed after Stoke's protests about the pitch conditions – the match was played in sleet on heavy ground – were upheld. Having lost the original match 4-0, Stoke then went on to lose the replayed match 8-0. This was the fourth time City had conceded eight or more in a game this season.

WEDNESDAY 22nd FEBRUARY 1922

Having beaten neighbours Port Vale and Northampton Town to reach the third round of the FA Cup, Stoke took Aston Villa to a replay. The game at Villa Park was a one-sided affair with the hosts running out comfortable 4-0 winners.

SATURDAY 22nd FEBRUARY 1992

The Potters regained top spot thanks to a Mark Stein tap-in against Brentford, who slipped from first to second in the Third Division. A gate of 16,417 ensured a good atmosphere as Macari's team set up a crunch match at St Andrew's against fellow high-flyers Birmingham.

SATURDAY 22ND FEBRUARY 2003

Marlon Harewood hit four goals and Petur Marteinsson was sent off as Stoke hit rock bottom in the First Division after a 6-0 defeat to Nottingham Forest at the City Ground. Tony Pulis' side seemed to be doomed to relegation.

SATURDAY 23RD FEBRUARY 1884

Teddy Johnson, Stoke's first international, won his second and final cap, scoring twice for England in the 8-1 demolition of Ireland in Belfast. The pacy and skilful winger only played one competitive match for the Potters – their first FA Cup tie against Manchester – before being forced to retire with a back injury.

SATURDAY 23RD FEBRUARY 1946

During the final year of wartime football, Stoke beat Blackpool 6-3 with Stanley Matthews starring against the team he would soon join. The other star of the match was Freddie Steele who scored four of Stoke's goals.

SATURDAY 23RD FEBRUARY 1957

Lincoln City were thrashed 8-0 with Neville 'Tim' Coleman scoring seven from the wing – still a record for a wing man – and Johnny King netted the other. Coleman's tally now stood at 26 for the season after only 32 games, and the result left Stoke third in the league. A run of only 6 points from the last ten games, and no goals for Coleman, left Stoke finishing fifth and Freddie Steele's goalscoring record from 1936/37 intact.

SATURDAY 23RD FEBRUARY 1974

Some 39,598 – the highest gate of the season – were at the Victoria Ground for the visit of Leeds United, who remained unbeaten after 29 games and held a nine point lead at the top of the table. Things looked bleak as Leeds took a 2-0 lead inside 20 minutes thanks to Bremner and Clarke, but Stoke were level by half time through Mike Pejic and Alan Hudson. In the second half Denis Smith rose to power home a header to win the match and end Leeds' unbeaten run.

SATURDAY 23RD FEBRUARY 1991

Immediately after a 4-0 defeat at Springfield Park, the home of Wigan Athletic, Alan Ball resigned as Stoke boss. The World Cup winner, whose father was once a coach at the club, bowed to increasing pressure. At times he used cotton wool in his ears to block out the abuse, but the displeasure of the supporters finally convinced him to quit. Ball left with a league record of just 15 wins in 58 matches in his time as manager.

SATURDAY 24TH FEBRUARY 1934

A brace from Joe Johnson gave Stoke a 2-1 victory at Villa Park in front of 25,000 fans. The victory was Stoke's first away to Aston Villa in the league, at the 20th attempt.

SATURDAY 24TH FEBRUARY 1940

Only 2,037 turned up at Edgeley Park to see Stockport County take on Stoke in the War League. The home fans did not have a good day as Stoke won 5-1 with a four-goal haul for Syd Peppitt.

SATURDAY 24TH FEBRUARY 1945

Port Vale were again on the receiving end of a heavy beating by Stoke in the War League Cup, this time by a 6-2 scoreline just seven days after an 8-1 defeat at the Victoria Ground. Freddie Steele scored a hat-trick, Tommy Sale two and Frankie Soo the other.

SATURDAY 25TH FEBRUARY 1899

At the fifth attempt, Stoke finally won an FA Cup quarter-final by beating Spurs 4-1 at the Victoria Ground in front of 22,000. The club's first semi-final would be against Derby County at Molineux.

SATURDAY 25TH FEBRUARY 1978

The visit of Bolton Wanderers ended in a 0-0 draw as new manager Alan Durban took over the reins from caretaker Alan A'Court. Durban was recruited from Shrewsbury Town, although the rumours were that Stoke wanted Bill McGarry of Newcastle United. His task was to return City to the First Division as soon as possible.

SATURDAY 25TH FEBRUARY 1984

Mark Chamberlain's early goal gave Stoke a third top-flight win in a row as the recovery continued since Bill Asprey's masterstroke of reuniting Alan Hudson with his adoring Potteries public. Hudson had rejoined Stoke from Chelsea again and he would stay for fifteen months before being forced to retire through injury. He played a significant part in the club's top flight survival battle in 1983/84.

SATURDAY 26TH FEBRUARY 1972

The FA Cup fifth round tie at home to Hull City was much easier than the previous year's quarter-final against the Tigers. Hull were beaten 4-1 with two goals from Jimmy Greenhoff and one each for Terry Conroy and John Ritchie in front of 34,558 at the Victoria Ground.

SATURDAY 26TH FEBRUARY 1994

Toddy Orlygsson and Martin Carruthers scored for Stoke as they beat Portsmouth 2-0 to hit fifth spot in the First Division table. Joe Jordan's men could not sustain this form and only four more wins in 14 matches left them with a tenth place finish at the end of the season.

WEDNESDAY 26TH FEBRUARY 2003

Stoke reacted well to a 6-0 drubbing by Nottingham Forest four days earlier by beating Walsall 1-0 thanks to Lee Mills' 19th-minute strike. The victory lifted City back off the bottom and started a revival.

THURSDAY 27TH FEBRUARY 1890

Near neighbours Crewe Alexandra were the opposition for Stoke's first floodlit match under temporary lights. The friendly played under 'Wells Lights' at the Victoria Ground was won by Stoke 3-1.

WEDNESDAY 27TH FEBRUARY 1991

Stoke travelled to Dean Court to take on AFC Bournemouth in the Third Division. Wayne Biggins gave Stoke the lead before John Butler was carried off on a stretcher after a poor challenge from future Stoke boss Tony Pulis. Mick Kennedy lost control and kicked a Cherries player to earn a red card as the Cherries scored three to win easily.

SATURDAY 27TH FEBRUARY 1993

Brisbane Road, the home of Leyton Orient, was the location for Stoke's record unbeaten run of 25 games to come to an end after a 1-0 defeat. The run stretched all the way back to early September.

SATURDAY 28TH FEBRUARY 1931

A goalless draw at home to Charlton Athletic, witnessed by less than 2,500 spectators, saw the final appearance in a Stoke shirt of Charlie Wilson. His total of 121 goals in 175 appearances was a record at the time, and his 38 league and Cup goals scored in 1926/27 was a club record which still stands today. Wilson moved to Stafford Rangers in June 1931.

SATURDAY 28TH FEBRUARY 1953

Playing his first game after an absence of nearly five months, Roy Brown netted twice as Stoke beat Manchester United 3-1, with James Martin getting the other. The visit of Matt Busby's Red Devils drew a crowd of 30,219 to the Victoria Ground. Stoke would win only three out of the next 11 matches as they failed to stave off relegation from the top flight in Frank Taylor's first season as manager.

SATURDAY 28TH FEBRUARY 1987

The visit to Fratton Park was not a happy one as Portsmouth ran out comfortable 3-0 winners in the Second Division. There was further bad news for Stoke as Brian Talbot was forced to leave the field injured, to be replaced by Chris Hemming. Hemming made national headlines when he had a pacemaker fitted, and yet was able to return to first team action. The Newcastle-under-Lyme-born defender went on to make 105 appearances for City, scoring two goals, before moving to Hereford United in August 1989 for £25,000.

SATURDAY 29TH FEBRUARY 1992

The Division Three clash between Stoke and Birmingham City at St. Andrews was played to a finish behind closed doors after serious crowd trouble. A Frain penalty had given Birmingham the lead but Stoke kept top spot thanks to a Paul Barnes equaliser in the last minute after Biggins had slid into Blues keeper Miller. Blues thought they had won it at the death, but when the goal was not given, the fans invaded the pitch.

SATURDAY 1st MARCH 1890

A hat-trick from Bob Ramsay, and two goals apiece for Charlie Baker and Harry Simpson, saw Stoke cruise to a 7-1 beating of Accrington at the Victoria Ground. The win was only the third of the season for Stoke and it kept them just above Burnley at the bottom of the table.

SATURDAY 1st MARCH 1924

South Shields came to Stoke and earned a point after a goalless draw in front of 8,348. The dropped point saw the Potters slip from first to third in the Second Division with ten games remaining in the season, as they were overtaken by Leeds United and Bury.

WEDNESDAY 1st MARCH 1978

Doncaster Rovers forward Brendan O'Callaghan signed for an initial fee of £40,000. He would not have to wait long to make a big impact on the side.

SATURDAY 2nd MARCH 1946

Stoke's record gate for a home FA Cup tie turned out to see the first leg of the quarter-final against Bolton Wanderers. The 50,735 present saw City go down 2-0, but as all ties were over two legs in this first post-war season, there was still a glimmer of hope for the second leg at Burnden Park.

SATURDAY 2nd MARCH 1957

Frank Taylor's Stoke team drew 1-1 – with George Kelly on the score-sheet – at Sheffield United to move into second place in the Second Division, six points behind the leaders Leicester City. However, they did not score any goals or take any points from the next six games and they dropped out of the promotion race finishing in fifth position.

SUNDAY 2nd MARCH 2008

The televised match at Loftus Road saw Stoke fail to regain top spot from Bristol City as Queens Park Rangers cruised to a 3-0 victory. Stoke's day was made even worse by the dismissal of captain Andy Griffin, whose red card was later rescinded by referee Andy D'Urso.

MONDAY 3RD MARCH 1902

Mart Watkins earned his first Welsh cap against England at Wrexham, in a match which finished goalless. Watkins had three spells at Stoke and earned a total of ten caps for Wales. The centre-forward initially joined Stoke from Oswestry Town in 1900 and finally left the club when he retired in 1914 having scored a total of 62 goals in 139 appearances.

SATURDAY 3RD MARCH 1923

As Stoke plunged back towards the Second Division, Arthur Shallcross resigned as manager. The final straw was the defeat to Burnley by the odd goal in five, with Stoke's strikes coming from Davies and Eyres. Shallcross had never been popular with the Stoke fans, despite winning promotion in 1922, as he had sold the popular Charlie Parker to Sunderland in 1920.

SATURDAY 3RD MARCH 1928

After beating Manchester City in the fifth round, Stoke made the trip to Arsenal in the FA Cup quarter-final. Despite Charlie Wilson's sixth goal of the season in the competition, Stoke were not good enough and Arsenal cruised through 4-1 in front of 41,974. The Potters have never beaten the Gunners in a cup match after 12 attempts, but they have fared better in the league, winning 20 and losing 36 out of the 74 matches played.

SATURDAY 3RD MARCH 1934

The FA Cup quarter-final saw City travel to Maine Road to face Manchester City in front of 84,569, a record crowd in England for a game outside of London. An error by goalkeeper Roy John proved costly as he let a cross from Eric Brook float directly into the net. This was enough to see the home side progress to the semi-finals.

FRIDAY 3RD MARCH 2000

The funeral took place of Sir Stanley Matthews, who had died on 23rd February. After a procession through the city his ashes were buried under the centre spot on the Britannia Stadium pitch.

SATURDAY 4TH MARCH 1972

The Potters' first visit to Wembley Stadium saw them come away with the League Cup – their first major trophy – after beating favourites Chelsea 2-1. A crowd of 97,852 saw Stoke take the lead after only five minutes through Terry Conroy, before Peter Osgood equalised just before half time. With 73 minutes gone George Eastham scored the winning goal, netting the rebound after Bonetti had parried Jimmy Greenhoff's shot. Stoke had to rely on some fine goalkeeping from Gordon Banks, particularly after a terrible back-pass from Mike Bernard put Baldwin through on goal. Waddo's men clung on to win and Peter Dobing lifted the trophy handed to him by Uefa President Gustav Wiederkehr at the top of the famous Wembley steps.

SATURDAY 4TH MARCH 2000

The home crowd was in mourning the death of Sir Stanley Matthews and Gudjon Thordarson's team did Stan's memory proud as they beat Chesterfield 5-1. Peter Thorne claimed four of the goals.

SATURDAY 5TH MARCH 1892

For England's 2-0 Home Championship victory over Ireland in Belfast, Stoke provided the defensive trio of Billy Rowley, Tommy Clare and Alf Underwood. This was the first occasion that three Stoke players had appeared in the same international side.

MONDAY 5TH MARCH 2001

Stoke fell to Port Vale at the quarter-final stage of the LDV Vans Trophy. This was the second time that eventual winners Vale had knocked the Potters out at this stage of the tournament.

WEDNESDAY 5TH MARCH 2003

A vital relegation battle with Brighton & Hove Albion took place at the Britannia Stadium. Chris Greenacre struck in the 83rd minute to send the majority of the 21,023 present wild with delight. The three points lifted the Potters above the Seagulls and out of the bottom three in the division. The relegation battle was a four-horse race with Sheffield Wednesday and Grimsby Town also in the thick of it.

WEDNESDAY 6TH MARCH 1963

The FA Cup third round tie at Elland Road, originally scheduled to be played on 5th January, finally went ahead after 12 postponements during the harsh 1963 winter. Leeds won the tie 3-1 with Keith Bebbington scoring for Stoke.

SATURDAY 6TH MARCH 1971

After a wait of 72 years Stoke finally made it into the FA Cup semi-finals for the second time in their history after beating Hull City 3-2 at Boothferry Park. The crowd of over 40,000 saw Stoke come back to win from two down with John Ritchie scoring twice in the last 20 minutes and Terry Conroy grabbing the other just before half-time. The victory set up a semi-final date with Bertie Mee's double-chasing Arsenal at Sheffield Wednesday's Hillsborough.

SATURDAY 7TH MARCH 1903

After Stoke had beaten Nottingham Forest in a replay, they travelled to Derby County in the FA Cup quarter-final in a repeat of the semi-final from four years previously. There was to be no revenge for that defeat as Derby were too strong for Stoke. Although only a point separated them towards the top of the First Division table, the Rams ran out 3-0 winners at the Baseball Ground.

SATURDAY 7TH MARCH 1908

The FA Cup quarter-final: the Potters' first time at this stage for five years pitched Stoke against their Staffordshire rivals Wolverhampton Wanderers at Molineux. In front of 31,800 supporters Wolves were victorious by the only goal of a tight game.

SATURDAY 7TH MARCH 1998

Second-from-bottom Huddersfield Town outplayed Stoke and easily won 2-1. This result combined with Port Vale's 3-0 win at Reading to send Stoke to the foot of the First Division table. Danny Tiatto scored in the last minute for Stoke, whose performance was so bad that the fans thought club mascot Pottermus could do better. This inspired the Boothen End to start chanting 'Bring on the Hippo'!

SATURDAY 8TH MARCH 1941

Walsall inflicted Stoke's second seven-goal defeat of the season in the Southern Regional League at Fellows Park. The Stoke goals in the 7-3 loss were scored by Frank Bowyer, Bobby Liddle and Eric Longland.

WEDNESDAY 8TH MARCH 1978

Big Brendan O'Callaghan scored with his first touch in a Stoke shirt, just 11 seconds after coming on as a substitute for Viv Busby. He was sent on when Stoke had won a corner and headed in Paul Richardson's cross. The only goal of the game in the 78th minute was enough to beat Hull City and 'Big Bren', recently signed from Doncaster Rovers, became an overnight hero for the Boothen Enders. O'Callaghan, who played both as a centre-forward and centre-half in his time with the Potters went on to make 294 appearances scoring 47 goals.

SATURDAY 9TH MARCH 1946

One of the blackest days in English football history. After losing the first leg of the FA Cup quarter-final 2-0 – all ties were over two legs in 1946/47 – Stoke were knocked out after goalless second leg against Bolton at Burnden Park. Although the official attendance was given as 65,419 some estimates put the actual figure as high as 85,000. As the two teams emerged the pressure of the crowd caused two barriers to collapse and the crush which followed killed 33 people and injured more than 400 others. The match was stopped after 12 minutes but later resumed to a finish. The Burnden Park disaster was one of the worst incidents of loss of life at a football ground.

TUESDAY 9TH MARCH 1993

Diminutive City striker Mark Stein landed himself in hot water after punching Stockport County's giant centre-half Jim Gannon. After a 2-1 result in Stoke's favour at the Victoria Ground, with Stein scoring the first, City's leading scorer reacted to racist abuse and the case ended up in court.

SATURDAY 10TH MARCH 1923

The first season back in the top flight after 15 years was proving to be tricky for the Potters and a 1-0 defeat at home to Burnley dropped them into the bottom two with only nine games to go. The match was the first under the stewardship of John Rutherford. The former Newcastle United, Arsenal and England winger's tenure lasted barely a month.

WEDNESDAY 10TH MARCH 1926

Outside-left Harry Oscroft, who played for Stoke for nearly a decade, was born in Mansfield. Sold to Stoke for £38,000, plus Verdi Godwin, by Mansfield Town in 1950 – who were under the management of former Stoke hero Freddie Steele – he turned himself into a fixture in the side and weighed in with his fair share of goals. After 349 appearances and 107 goals he moved across the city to Port Vale as part of an exchange deal for Dickie Cunliffe.

MONDAY 10TH MARCH 1958

Future BBC football pundit Garth Crooks was born in Stoke. Legend has it that Crooks was signed by Tony Waddington after he saw him kicking a ball against a wall outside the Victoria Ground. The striker went on to play for Stoke, Spurs, West Bromwich Albion, Charlton Athletic and Manchester United before retiring to concentrate on media work in 1995. He won back-to-back FA Cup winners' medals whilst at Tottenham and was awarded an OBE in 1999.

SATURDAY 11TH MARCH 1933

Stoke slipped to second place in the Second Division table on goals scored behind Tottenham Hotspur after a 2-0 defeat at home to Notts County in front of 14,223.

WEDNESDAY 11TH MARCH 1992

Despite a 2-1 home defeat at the hands of relegation-threatened Bury, City remained at the top of the Second Division. Ian Stevens did the damage with two second-half goals for the Shakers. The gap at the top of the table was now four points over third-placed West Bromwich Albion.

SATURDAY 12TH MARCH 1927

The derby game at the Victoria Ground against Crewe Alexandra finished 2-1 in Stoke's favour thanks to goals from John Eyres and Arty Watkin. The crowd of 16,827 saw Stoke increase the gap over their Third Division (North) promotion rivals from four to five points. The chasing pack was made up of Bradford Park Avenue, Halifax Town, Nelson and Rochdale, all of whom could still catch Stoke.

SATURDAY 12TH MARCH 1932

Stoke slipped to fifth place in the Second Division after a 4-3 home defeat at the hands of Leeds United in front of around 8,500. Bobby Liddle suffered an eye injury during the match which paved the way for the debut of 17-year-old Stanley Matthews in the next game. Matthews only played two games all season.

SATURDAY 12TH MARCH 1938

Arthur Turner's appearance in the 3-1 defeat to Blackpool was his 128th consecutive game, a club record only broken once since then.

MONDAY 13TH MARCH 1893

The Victoria Ground hosted its second England international match, four years after the first. The game, like the first, was against Wales. The score in the first fixture was 4-1 to the home side, but on this occasion it was 6-0. The ground would host one more international.

SATURDAY 13TH MARCH 1926

In a last ditch attempt to avoid the drop into Division Three, Stoke had signed Charlie Wilson from Herbert Chapman's all-conquering Huddersfield Town side. On his debut he could do nothing to prevent a 4-0 defeat at Clapton Orient as Stoke slipped further into the mire.

SATURDAY 13TH MARCH 1954

City's biggest-ever away win came at Gigg Lane against Bury in the Second Division. Two goals each for Frank Bowyer and Harry Oscroft, one for Johnny King and an own goal from Hart gave Stoke a 6-0 victory and left the Potters lying tenth in the table.

SATURDAY 14TH MARCH 1896

After losing 5-2 at Aston Villa, Stoke bounced back well by beating Sunderland in their next league match at the Victoria Ground. Stoke scored five without reply thanks to Willy Maxwell, Allan Maxwell, Billy Heames, Tom Hyslop from the penalty spot and a McNeil own goal. Allan Maxwell's goal came on his home debut after moving to Stoke from Darwen, with a set of wrought iron gates for the Lancashire club's ground going in the opposite direction as the transfer fee! Allan Maxwell, who had scored a goal every three games for both Everton and Darwen, could only muster six in 37 appearances for Stoke despite the good start. He left for St. Bernard's Edinburgh just a year later.

SATURDAY 14TH MARCH 1925

With only nine games left to go Stoke hit the foot of the Second Division for the first time and there was a real danger of Third Division football at the Victoria Ground. A crowd of 20,000 had turned out to see the 3-0 defeat to Wolves.

SATURDAY 14TH MARCH 1987

The 2-1 defeat at Ewood Park had further reaching consequences than simply the loss of three points. The back injury sustained in the match by Steve Bould would keep him out of action for six months. The resulting loss of form by the Potters would cost them a play-off place at the end of the season.

TUESDAY 14TH MARCH 2000

The first leg of the Auto Windscreens Shield semi-final at Spotland saw Stoke win 3-1, giving Rochdale an uphill task in the second leg. Peter Thorne scored two of the goals and Mikael Hansson got the other.

MONDAY 15TH MARCH 1880

The Wales versus England match at Wrexham saw the first-ever international call-up for a Stoke player. Centre-forward Teddy Johnson played in England's 3-2 victory, but he had to wait four years for his second and final cap.

PETER THORNE SCORED TWICE FOR STOKE AT ROCHDALE IN MARCH 2000

SATURDAY 15TH MARCH 1952

Norman Wilkinson played his last game aged 41 years and 275 days, after 17 years service, against his first club, Huddersfield Town.

SATURDAY 15TH MARCH 2008

A dour goalless draw at Watford saw Stoke regain top spot in the Championship from Bristol City on goal difference. Despite ex-Potter John Eustace being sent off, Watford were the better side and on-loan Carlo Nash saved a penalty to earn the point. The fight for the top flight was a race against Bristol City, Watford and West Bromwich Albion.

SATURDAY 16TH MARCH 1918

An large crowd of 16,000 were at the Victoria Ground for the visit of Burnley as Stoke closed in on the Lancashire Section Championship. They went away happy as Stoke ran out 9-0 winners to clinch their place in the Championship Final against Leeds City.

SATURDAY 16TH MARCH 1974

Southampton striker Peter Osgood, once a Stoke target, had criticised John Ritchie's ability – except with his head – in the build up to the match. Ritchie went on to score a hat-trick and for the third he stopped the ball on the line, knelt down, and headed it in. The 4-1 score was completed by Geoff Hurst with his 200th league goal.

WEDNESDAY 17TH MARCH 1890

A point away at Aston Villa was not enough to prevent Stoke being confirmed as wooden spoon winners for the second year in succession. With a game left, Burnley were now out of reach. Stoke were not re-elected and left the Football League to join the Football Alliance for one season, with Sunderland taking their place.

MONDAY 17TH MARCH 1965

On his 24th birthday, Harry Burrows signed for £27,000 from Aston Villa, where he had fallen out with new manager Dick Taylor over his contract terms. Burrows stayed at Stoke for eight years and in the process racked up 281 appearances and 79 goals from outside-left.

SATURDAY 18TH MARCH 1899

A first-half goal from Willie Maxwell put Stoke in front, but was not enough to prevent defeat in the club's first FA Cup semi-final against Derby County. The game, played at Molineux in front of a 20,000 crowd, was won thanks to a hat-trick from Steve Bloomer after the Rams had weathered some intense Stoke pressure.

SATURDAY 18TH MARCH 1911

Wrexham exacted revenge on Stoke by beating them 7-1 in the Birmingham League, in front of a crowd of just 3,000. Stoke had beaten the Welsh side 6-2 earlier in the season at the Victoria Ground.

SATURDAY 19TH MARCH 1932

A promising outside-right by the name of Stanley Matthews made his debut away at Bury in place of Bobby Liddle. Stoke won thanks to a goal from Maloney and moved up to third in the Division Two table.

SATURDAY 19TH MARCH 1977

Forced to sell many of his better players to raise money for the ground, Tony Waddington was starting to feel the pressure at the helm as he saw a last-minute goal from Frank Worthington, a one-time Stoke target, clinch victory for Leicester City at the 'Vic'.

SATURDAY 19TH MARCH 1983

Steve Bould scored a spectacular own goal at Upton Park by lobbing Peter Fox from distance. The match ended 1-1 against West Ham United thanks to Mickey Thomas' finish from Mark Chamberlain's run. Bould's effort won 'Own Goal of the Season' on ITV's *Saint & Greavsie*.

SATURDAY 20TH MARCH 1954

Bill Asprey started his long association with Stoke City as he made his debut away to Oldham Athletic, where he replaced Frank Mountford in the starting eleven. It would take another three years before he established himself as a first-team regular, but the versatile defender would go on to score 26 goals in 341 appearances for the club. In the mid-eighties he would return for a very unhappy spell as manager.

SATURDAY 20TH MARCH 1993

Bruce Grobbelaar made his Stoke debut and a Mark Stein penalty was enough to beat Fulham and keep City ten points clear at the top of the Second Division. Stein had a fantastic record for the Potters scoring 72 goals in 134 games.

SATURDAY 21ST MARCH 1964

Stoke boosted their survival hopes by trouncing bottom-of-the-table Ipswich Town 9-1 at the Victoria Ground. The result put Stoke nine points clear with nine games to play. Dennis Viollet scored a hat-trick, Jimmy McIlroy and John Ritchie scored two each and Peter Dobing and Keith Bebbington scored the others.

SATURDAY 21ST MARCH 1987

Stoke drew 2-2 away to Huddersfield Town thanks to goals from Tony Ford and Keith Bertschin. This started a run of five consecutive draws, a club record.

SATURDAY 21ST MARCH 1998

At the 12th attempt Chris Kamara finally won as Stoke manager. The 2-1 win at home to QPR came thanks to an Iain Dowie own goal and a Dean Crowe effort. Kamara brought in plenty of new players – including Kyle Lightbourne for a club record £500,000 – and a total of 29 were used in those 12 games alone.

WEDNESDAY 22ND MARCH 1972

The FA Cup quarter-final replay was the fifth time Stoke had faced Manchester United in cup competitions that season. Having already knocked the Old Trafford side out of the League Cup, the Potters now ended United's FA Cup hopes too. The crowd of 49,091 was the third highest cup gate ever at the Victoria Ground, and the tie went into extra time after Denis Smith had cancelled out George Best's opener. Smith had been ruled out before the match with a bad back, but played after it clicked back into place walking to the ground from his car! Terry Conroy hit the winner to send Stoke to their third semi-final against the previous year's semi-final opponents Arsenal.

TUESDAY 22ND MARCH 1977

The *Evening Sentinel* said it all, 'I Quit – Tony Waddington'. The most successful manager in the club's history had tendered his resignation which had been accepted by chairman Albert Henshall. 'Waddo', whose salary of £25,000 was one of the highest in the league, had been in charge for nearly 17 years, had overseen nearly 900 competitive games, won the club's only piece of silverware, and brought European football to the Potteries. In league football Stoke played 701 games under Waddo of which they won 241, drew 197 and lost 263. In cup football Stoke played 144 games, winning 61, drawing 42 and losing 41. Tony Waddington died in Crewe in 1994.

WEDNESDAY 22ND MARCH 2000

Peter Thorne scored the only goal of the game to send Stoke to Wembley in the Auto Windscreens Shield. Nearly 17,000 fans were there to see the victory over Rochdale by a 4-1 aggregate score. Stoke City would meet Bristol City in the final.

SATURDAY 23RD MARCH 1878

The Stoke club, having dropped the Ramblers suffix and now playing their home games at Sweeting's Field, became the inaugural winners of the Staffordshire Cup beating Talke Rangers 1-0. In an earlier round they had beaten Mow Cop by an all-competition club record score of 26-0. Stoke's first team played in the Staffordshire Cup until 1914/15.

WEDNESDAY 23RD MARCH 1977

The day after Tony Waddington quit the club, George Eastham took temporary charge of Stoke for the visit of high-flying Arsenal. Despite the 2-0 defeat thanks to goals from Pat Rice and Malcolm MacDonald, Eastham enjoyed the experience enough to eventually apply for and get the manager's job on a more permanent basis.

SATURDAY 23RD MARCH 2002

On-loan Icelandic international Arnar Gunnlaugsson hit a sweet left foot volley to beat Chesterfield. The 23rd-minute strike was witnessed by 14,841 spectators. Gunnlaugsson scored 6 goals in his 29 Stoke games.

MONDAY 24TH MARCH 1890

The last game of the second season of the Football League not only saw Stoke say farewell to the league for 12 months, it was also the end for their manager Harry Lockett. Lockett relinquished his duties at Stoke to concentrate on his role at the Football League of which he was secretary from their offices in Etruria.

SATURDAY 24TH MARCH 1928

A hat-trick from Charlie Wilson helped Stoke to a 5-1 victory over Fulham at the Victoria Ground. Fulham, above only Gainsborough Trinity, were no match for the Potters whose other two goals came from a Len Armitage penalty and Harry Davies. A 10,117 crowd saw Stoke keep alive their hopes of back-to-back promotions being five points behind the leading pack with eight games left.

MONDAY 25TH MARCH 1895

Stoke drew 1-1 at home to West Bromwich Albion thanks to a Dickson goal. After the match Stoke went on their longest run of consecutive league victories, which totalled nine and ran until the end of September.

SATURDAY 25TH MARCH 1972

A crowd of 33,593 were at the Victoria Ground for the visit of Brian Clough's Derby County. Jimmy Greenhoff put City ahead from the penalty spot at the start of the second half before Stoke manager-to-be Alan Durban equalised midway through the half. Derby had a goal disallowed as Stoke hung on for a point leaving Cloughie's Rams in second.

FRIDAY 26TH MARCH 1937

Highbury Stadium witnessed the end of a great Stoke City career as Harry Davies played his last game in a Stoke shirt. Davies, who scored a goal every four games with the Potters, could not manage one against Arsenal as the two teams played out a goalless draw. Davies scored 101 goals in two spells at the Victoria Ground, leaving first for Huddersfield Town in 1929 and then Port Vale in 1938 after a year in Stoke's reserves.

SATURDAY 26TH MARCH 1960

A small crowd of 6,223 were at the Victoria Ground to see a disappointing 3-1 defeat to Scunthorpe United, with Johnny King bagging Stoke's goal. The match marked a real end of an era at Stoke as John McCue made his final appearance in the famous red and white stripes nearly 20 years after his first. Including wartime football, the Stoke-born full-back made 675 appearances scoring two goals. He represented Stoke for 23 years before moving on to play for a further three years at Oldham Athletic and Macclesfield Town. McCue died in Longton, his birthplace, in 1999.

SATURDAY 27TH MARCH 1937

Sunderland were the visitors on Easter Saturday as City ran out 5-3 winners in front of nearly 30,000 Stokies. Stoke's goals came from Jim Westland, Arthur Tutin and a hat-trick from Freddie Steele. The hat-trick was one of five Steele scored that season on his way to a club record haul of 33 league goals.

WEDNESDAY 27TH MARCH 1963

Tony Allen set a club record by playing is his 136th consecutive match at home to Swansea Town. His run in the side had started three years previously at Hull City's Boothferry Park.

SATURDAY 27TH MARCH 1971

There was heartbreak for all of the Stoke fans in the 54,770 crowd at the FA Cup semi-final at Hillsborough. Stoke were leading 2-0 at half time through Denis Smith and John Ritchie. John Mahoney handled the ball on the line in the sixth minute of injury time and Peter Storey scored from the spot to earn Arsenal a replay.

THURSDAY 28TH MARCH 1878

A friendly match against Talke Rangers, which Stoke won 1-0, was the first match to be played at the Victoria Athletic Club Ground. A merger between Stoke and the Stoke Victoria Athletic Club had instigated the move from Sweeting's Field to what would later be renamed the Victoria Ground.

SATURDAY 28TH MARCH 1925

Stoke pulled off a 2-1 victory at home to Portsmouth to lift themselves off the bottom of the table. The crowd of 9,920 was half that for the previous home game against Wolves, but Joe Clennell and Dick Johnson got the all-important goals, with both players being recruited in February to do just that.

FRIDAY 29TH MARCH 1907

A 1-0 defeat to Newcastle United at St James' Park in front of 30,000 left Stoke four points adrift at the bottom of the First Division with just six games left to play.

MONDAY 29TH MARCH 1937

A goalless draw with league leaders Arsenal on Easter Monday was witnessed by a record home crowd of 51,373 at the Victoria Ground.

SATURDAY 30TH MARCH 1929

Charlie Wilson scored two as Stoke beat Middlesbrough by the odd goal in five. The result left City fourth with six games left and in with a chance of a return to the First Division. Unfortunately, Stoke would only win two more games all season and would finish sixth. It would be four more years before a return to the top flight.

WEDNESDAY 30TH MARCH 1960

The smallest home league crowd since World War Two was at the Victoria Ground to see a 2-1 defeat at the hands of Ipswich Town. Only 4,070 turned out to see the Second Division match in which Dennis Wilshaw scored the Stoke goal.

SATURDAY 30TH MARCH 1985

Heading for relegation from the top division, Stoke won only their third game of the season beating Arsenal 2-0 thanks to goals from Ian Painter and Paul Dyson. These would be the last points collected that season as City went on a run of defeats which stretched into the next season. The run totalled 11 matches, a club record, and would leave Stoke with only three wins, 17 points, and 24 goals scored all season.

WEDNESDAY 31st MARCH 1971

After coming so close to Wembley in the original tie, Stoke were never in the FA Cup semi-final replay at Villa Park. The Potters went down 2-0 in front of 62,356, with Arsenal going on to win the double, beating Liverpool in the final.

MONDAY 31st MARCH 1975

A crowd of 45,954 saw Terry Conroy score both goals in a 2-0 victory at home to Liverpool. The result kept Stoke in fifth and left them in pole position for the league title with only four games left. After the match Liverpool boss Bill Shankly entered the City dressing room, shook Alan Hudson by the hand and said that it was the best 90 minutes of football he had ever seen!

SATURDAY 31st MARCH 1979

A 2-1 reverse at home to Blackburn Rovers was the second home defeat in four days. The dip in form saw Stoke drop out of the promotion places for the first time all season.

WEDNESDAY 31st MARCH 1993

The Potteries derby was a top versus second encounter as Lou Macari's table-topping Stoke travelled to Vale Park to face John Rudge's Port Vale side. The Potters led early on as John Butler jinked down the right wing and centred for Mark Stein to slam the ball home. Stoke were never really in trouble after that and Nigel Gleghorn added a second after the break. Stoke looked to be certainties for promotion.

SATURDAY 1st APRIL 1972

The Jackie Trent and Tony Hatch penned 'We'll Be With You', recorded by The Potters for the League Cup Final, entered the pop charts. The single stayed for two weeks and peaked at number 34, although it did not receive much national radio airplay.

MONDAY 1st APRIL 2002

After beating Swindon Town 2-0, Stoke were only five points adrift of second place in the Second Division. Wayne Thomas and Chris Iwelumo scored to give the Potters a glimmer of hope for an automatic promotion spot to the First Division in the last three games.

SATURDAY 2nd APRIL 1898

Willie Maxwell, Stoke's centre-forward, earned his only cap for Scotland against England, and so he became the last man to earn a full Scottish cap whilst at Stoke. Maxwell was a fine player and goalscorer whose six years at Stoke yielded 85 goals in 173 games.

SATURDAY 2nd APRIL 1927

Second-placed Rochdale narrowed Stoke's lead at the top of the Division Three (North) table to just four points thanks to a 4-0 victory at Spotland. With just seven games to go, Stoke's last three league defeats had all come at the hands of their closest promotion rivals.

SUNDAY 3rd APRIL 1910

Former Stoke goalkeeper Dr Leigh Richmond Roose turned out against his old club's reserve side as a guest for Port Vale. With Stoke losing 2-0 late on the crowd invaded the pitch and picked up Roose, carrying him off towards the River Trent. The match was abandoned after the police and stewards intervened. Dr Roose was eventually released unharmed by the fans, and the result was made to stand.

FRIDAY 3rd APRIL 1931

Stoke's drift towards mid-table mediocrity in the Second Division was interrupted with a 7-3 defeat at Reading. The Stoke goals came courtesy of two from Wilf Kirkham and a Len Armitage spot kick.

FRIDAY 3RD APRIL 1992

After beating Darlington 3-0 at the Victoria Ground, Stoke were now six points clear of third place in the Third Division with only five games remaining. A brace for Wayne Biggins and one for Mark Stein – taking the combined league total for the strike pairing to 34 for the season – was enough to see off the bottom-of-the-table Quakers.

SATURDAY 4TH APRIL 1891

On the last day of the season, Stoke beat Sheffield Wednesday 5-1 to claim the Football Alliance title by three points from Sunderland Albion. For the 1891/92 season, Stoke returned to the Football League after being elected to the expanded fourteen-team league.

SATURDAY 4TH APRIL 1936

Arthur Turner and Stanley Matthews scored the goals which beat Everton at the Victoria Ground. Stoke were having a fantastic season and the win moved them up to third in the table, although a tilt at the title was never really a possibility as Sunderland were so far ahead.

FRIDAY 4TH APRIL 1947

Freddie Steele's hat-trick in the 5-2 victory at Grimsby Town took him past Charlie Wilson as the club's leading league goalscorer of all time. The victory started a run of seven successive victories which would put Stoke City in pole position for their first Football League title.

WEDNESDAY 4TH APRIL 1979

Two quick-fire goals from Denis Smith and Paul Randall were enough to beat Fulham at the Victoria Ground in front of 15,243 fans. The win lifted Stoke back into the top three promotion positions as the tension mounted at the top of Division Two.

SATURDAY 4TH APRIL 1998

A 2-0 reverse at Reading prompted Chris Kamara to resign from his job as manager after just 14 games in charge which had yielded only one win and eight points. Caretaker manager Alan Durban now had just five games to try to stave off impending relegation to the Second Division.

MONDAY 5TH APRIL 1915

Stoke clinched the Southern League Division Two title thanks to a 10-0 thumping of Ebbw Vale. Arty Watkin scored five in the match, whilst Alf Smith notched four and Dicky Smith got the other.

SATURDAY 5TH APRIL 1924

Jimmy Broad, Harry Sellars and Billy Tempest were all on the score-sheet as Stoke beat Manchester United 3-0 in front of 20,000 happy fans at the Victoria Ground. The victory kept promotion hopes alive as, with only five games left, Tom Mather's side were three points adrift of the Second Division promotion places.

SATURDAY 5TH APRIL 1947

On Easter Saturday, Stoke beat Huddersfield Town 3-0 at the Victoria Ground. A day earlier, the Potters had travelled to Grimsby Town and earned a 5-2 victory courtesy of a Freddie Steele hat-trick. These two results moved Stoke up into third place, five points behind the leaders Blackpool but with four games in hand giving City their best-ever chance of winning the league title.

SATURDAY 5TH APRIL 1975

In one of the closest First Division finishes ever, Stoke were one of four teams level on points at the top after a 3-0 victory over Chelsea. Terry Conroy scored twice as City cruised past the young Chelsea team to pull themselves level on 47 points with Liverpool, Derby County and Everton.

SATURDAY 5TH APRIL 2008

Crystal Palace raced into a two-goal lead at the Britannia Stadium as the form team in the Championship visited Stoke. Despite heavy second-half pressure Stoke could not get level, although Glenn Whelan did score his first goal since joining in January for £500,000 from Sheffield Wednesday. The poor run of form that meant Stoke had only won one in the last 8 matches appeared to be jeopardising any chance of automatic promotion. The Premiership race was hotting up as there were now five teams separated by only three points.

SATURDAY 6TH APRIL 1889

A 1-1 draw against Derby County, combined with other results, left Stoke at the bottom of the league on goal average. Notts County had completed their fixtures, so Stoke knew that a point was needed from their last match against Accrington to save them from receiving the wooden spoon in the first Football League season.

SATURDAY 6TH APRIL 1963

Stoke's sixth consecutive league victory saw them hit the top of the Second Division. The goals at Fratton Park which defeated Portsmouth were scored by Jackie Mudie, Don Ratcliffe and new signing from Burnley Jimmy McIlroy.

MONDAY 6TH APRIL 1992

The first leg of the Autoglass Trophy semi-final saw Peterborough United visit the Victoria Ground for a thrilling game. Wayne Biggins twice and Lee Sandford were on the score sheet to ensure the second leg for a place at Wembley would start with the sides level at 3-3.

MONDAY 7TH APRIL 1947

A fantastic Easter period continued for the Potters as they claimed their third victory in four days. A crowd of 34,269 saw Grimsby Town beaten thanks to two strikes from Johnny Jackson and one from Alec Ormston. The victory closed the gap on leaders Blackpool to just three points with Stoke having four games in hand on the Tangerines. John Jackson had possibly the best-ever league scoring ratio for Stoke as he notched three goals in just four appearances.

SATURDAY 7TH APRIL 2007

A magical three-goal burst in eight minutes gave Stoke the three points at the Hawthorns. West Bromwich Albion had no answer as Stoke swept up the field to score through Ricardo Fuller, a Jonathan Greening own goal and a Jon Parkin – who was on loan from Hull City – strike. With the match dead and buried, the Baggies pulled a goal back through Jason Koumas late on. With only five games to go, Stoke's play-off dreams were well and truly alive.

SATURDAY 8TH APRIL 1911

Bert Savage scored a hat-trick in Stoke's 10-0 demolition of Halesowen in the Birmingham League, yet he was outdone by Alf Smith who scored five! Smith scored 72 goals in his two spells at City at the rate of a goal every two games. He was described as being a good dribbler of the ball who was a real supporters' favourite.

SATURDAY 8TH APRIL 1916

Chesterfield Town visited Stoke during the Lancashire Secondary Competition in the war. A crowd of 7,000 saw Billy Herbert score a hat-trick in a 7-1 win. In total, including war football, Herbert scored 92 goals in his 202 appearances for the club. He was also one of only a few players to play for Stoke before, during and after the war.

MONDAY 8TH APRIL 1985

Former Stoke full-back Bill Asprey was sacked as manager after a humiliating 4-0 defeat at home to Luton Town, who were also struggling at the bottom. Tony Lacey took temporary charge until the end of the season. Asprey had only won 14 of his 60 games in the hotseat.

SATURDAY 9TH APRIL 1898

A 2-0 home victory against Everton, thanks to goals from Willie Maxwell and Fred Molyneux lifted Stoke out of the Test Match places. Stoke had finished their fixtures but both Bury and Blackburn Rovers beneath them had a game remaining. Victories for both left Stoke bottom and in the end-of-season Test Matches again.

TUESDAY 9TH APRIL 1901

A 2-0 victory at Wolves lifted Stoke out of the bottom two places on goal average and they knew that a win on the last day against Notts County would see them safe. Stoke won 4-2 against the Magpies and retained their top-flight status.

SATURDAY 9TH APRIL 1932

The 3-2 win over Plymouth Argyle saw Stoke move up to third place with only four matches remaining, giving them hope of promotion.

SATURDAY 9th APRIL 1983

Richie Barker's Stoke side moved into fifth place with just six games remaining and had given themselves a real chance of claiming a European spot. Struggling Manchester City came to defend but were beaten by a Sammy McIlroy effort after 61 minutes. The Potters' European ambitions were shattered as they took only three points from a possible 18 to finish up in the bottom half of the table.

MONDAY 10th APRIL 1922

Frank Bowyer was born in Chesterton. The inside-forward went on to play for Stoke for 21 years before joining Macclesfield Town in 1960.

SATURDAY 10th APRIL 1965

John Ritchie took his tally for the season to 26 goals by scoring all four as Stoke beat Sheffield Wednesday at the Victoria Ground. The result virtually ensured City stayed in the top flight as it left them ten points clear of the drop zone with only five games left to play.

SATURDAY 11th APRIL 1925

Survival hopes were boosted with a 3-1 victory at home to Blackpool in front of 15,912 fans. The match marked the last appearance of Tom Brittleton at the age of 46, having only joined when he was 41. The former England international had made 123 appearances in that time.

SATURDAY 11th APRIL 1987

With time slipping away to mount a challenge for a play-off place, Stoke had yet another draw; a club record fifth in a row. On this occasion it was a goalless encounter against high-flying Derby County. The sequence of draws would eventually end any lingering play-off hopes as City would finish eighth, six points adrift of fifth.

FRIDAY 11th APRIL 2008

BBC Radio Stoke's John Acres first broadcast Pottermouth's Battle Cry on his phone-in show. The inspirational message quickly became a symbol of the battle for the Premiership and, when put to pictures, rapidly became one of the BBC's most viewed items on YouTube.

MONDAY 12TH APRIL 1897

Stoke beat Bury thanks to a Darroch own goal and strikes from Hill and Joe Schofield to continue their fight against relegation. The run of three wins from the last three matches – the other two being against Blackburn Rovers and Sheffield United – was enough to lift the Potters to First Division safety.

SATURDAY 12TH APRIL 1947

A trip to league leaders Blackpool saw Alec Ormston and George Mountford give City a vital 2-0 victory. Although Stoke were lying in fourth position, they were only two points from the summit with just six games remaining.

SATURDAY 12TH APRIL 1975

With echoes of 1947, it's at Bramall Lane, in front of 33,255 fans, where Stoke's title challenge falters. The recently sustained broken legs to Denis Smith – for the fifth time in his career – Mike Pejic and Jimmy Robertson, finally appeared to have caught up with City. Sheffield United ran out 2-0 winners thanks to Keith Eddy and Anthony Field. In the end the Potters finished four points behind champions Derby County.

TUESDAY 12TH APRIL 1977

Garth Crooks scored twice at home to Leeds United to give Stoke the points, despite the visitors' domination. The win was George Eastham's first in his fifth game in charge, and it lifted Stoke to 14th in the table with only eight games remaining. It would be the last win of the season as the Potters slid dramatically towards Division Two for the first time in 14 years.

SATURDAY 12TH APRIL 2008

Coventry City's new Ricoh Arena saw the start of a fine run of form for Stoke which would see them promoted to the FA Premier League. Trailing 1-0 at half-time, Ricardo Fuller pulled a goal back after referee Uriah Rennie had pointed to the spot. Liam Lawrence came off the bench to volley the winner and celebrate his return from injury, which coincided with City's return to form.

LIAM LAWRENCE CELEBRATES HIS WINNER AT COVENTRY IN APRIL 2008

SATURDAY 13TH APRIL 1901

Stoke survived in Division One after a thrilling 4-2 victory at Notts County, avoiding relegation thanks to a second successive away win. Preston North End lost at home to the bottom side West Bromwich Albion, who then in turn lost all of their last three matches. Stoke's goals at Meadow Lane were scored by Sam Higginson, Mart Watkins, Fred Johnson and Willie Maxwell.

SATURDAY 13TH APRIL 1912

Millwall Athletic visited the Victoria Ground in the Southern League and were soundly beaten 7-0 thanks to a hat-trick from John Lenaghan, two from Alf Smith and one from Tommy Revill.

SATURDAY 13TH APRIL 1968

A sixth successive defeat completed City's plunge from mid-table safety in the First Division to the relegation places in a short space of time. The latest defeat, 2-0 at home to Wolves, would not be the last as the poor run of form would extend to no win in nine matches.

SATURDAY 13TH APRIL 1996

With only five games remaining, Stoke clawed their way in to the play-off positions with a win at Portsmouth. Pompey played 70 minutes with only ten men but it took until the last minute for Mike Sheron to score the decisive goal to take the points. Sheron had arrived at the Victoria Ground from Norwich City in a swap deal with Keith Scott and would be sold in July 1997 to Queens Park Rangers for £2.75m, having scored 39 goals in 76 appearances. His partnership with Simon Sturridge, dubbed the SAS, was a potent one which registered 28 league goals in 1995/96.

SATURDAY 13TH APRIL 2002

In the penultimate game of the season Stoke beat Wrexham 1-0, thanks to an Andy Cooke goal, in front of 14,298. The three points secured a play-off berth for the third successive season, although Stoke's opponents in the battle for a First Division place would not be known until after the final match.

MONDAY 14TH APRIL 1902

A win in the penultimate game of the season ensured Stoke's survival in their perennial battle against relegation during the early years of the Football League. Grimsby Town were beaten 2-0 with goals from Tom Holford and Mart Watkins to ensure a further year in the First Division.

THURSDAY 14TH APRIL 1910

Stoke beat Salisbury City 2-0 to achieve a 100% record for the ten game Southern League season, scoring 48 and conceding nine. Stoke also took part in the Birmingham League in this season, winning 17 and losing ten of the 34 games.

SATURDAY 14TH APRIL 1923

The second league win in succession – a 1-0 victory over Newcastle United, having beaten relegation rivals Nottingham Forest 1-0 a week previously – gave Stoke a faint hope of avoiding the drop back into the Second Division at the first time of asking. With three games to go the Potters were two points adrift of Chelsea and three behind Forest with a game in hand. Unfortunately, two of those last three games were against league leaders Liverpool.

MONDAY 14TH APRIL 1941

For the third time in the 1940/41 wartime season, Stoke conceded seven goals, on this occasion to Northampton Town in a 7-0 defeat. The other drubbings were a 7-2 loss at Mansfield Town and a 7-3 reverse at Wrexham.

SATURDAY 14TH APRIL 1984

League leaders and eventual champions Liverpool came to Stoke as the Potters continued their fight against relegation. A crowd of over 24,000 saw Ian Painter and Colin Russell win it for Bill Asprey's Stoke team. Alan Hudson orchestrated a period of keep-ball which frustrated the visitors to such an extent that Kenny Dalglish got himself booked and Graham Souness punched a window as he left the pitch! City had now won eight out of the 12 matches since Hudson's return having only won three out of the 24 prior to that.

MONDAY 15TH APRIL 1907

Albert Sturgess and Jackie Chalmers scored to give Stoke a 2-0 victory over Woolwich Arsenal. The win took Stoke's tally to three wins and a draw in their last four games. They were now only two points adrift of safety with two to play and a slim chance of staying up.

WEDNESDAY 15TH APRIL 1964

The first leg of the League Cup final saw a 1-1 draw at the 'Vic', with a goal from Keith Bebbington. Leicester City levelled through Dave Gibson.

FRIDAY 15TH APRIL 1972

For the second year running Hillsborough, with a crowd of 56,570, was the venue for the FA Cup semi-final against Arsenal, and for the second year running it would need to go to a replay. City took advantage of an injury to Bob Wilson to equalise through an own goal and then Peter Dobing hit the inside of the post with stand-in goalkeeper Radford having no chance.

SATURDAY 15TH APRIL 1989

Paul Ware gave Stoke all three points against the run of play at Dean Court after a Gerry Peyton mistake. The victory against AFC Bournemouth would be the last for six months as Stoke embarked on a run of 17 games without a win, the worst in the club's history. The fans were stunned as news of the Hillsborough tragedy filtered through.

WEDNESDAY 15TH APRIL 1992

London Road was packed with 12,214 supporters for the second leg of the Autoglass Trophy semi-final after a 3-3 draw at Stoke. Peterborough United were beaten by a tremendous Paul Ware free-kick in front of the Stoke fans. Next stop Wembley Stadium.

SATURDAY 16TH APRIL 1932

A point was not all that City took from Ashton Gate after a 0-0 draw. The Bristol City directors asked the visitors to take the pick of their squad and Stoke signed Joe Johnson for £250. Outside-left Johnson made 184 appearances for the Potters and earned five England caps.

MONDAY 16TH APRIL 1990

Newcastle United won 3-0 at St James' Park on Easter Monday to relegate Stoke City to the Third Division for the first time in 63 years, and only the second time in the club's history. Mick Quinn scored his 35th goal of the season for Newcastle, which is more than Stoke had managed as a team. The Stoke fans present displayed their feelings by singing: "We're not bothered any more!"

SATURDAY 17TH APRIL 1926

A 3-1 defeat at home to Chelsea, with Charlie Wilson netting Stoke's goal, dropped the Potters into the relegation places at the bottom of the Second Division for the first time all season with only three games to go.

SATURDAY 17TH APRIL 1937

England's visit to Hampden Park to play Scotland took on an extra significance in the Potteries as Stoke provided three forwards for the England side. Stanley Matthews, Freddie Steele and Joe Johnson all played in the 3-1 defeat in front of 149,547, which was a world record attendance. Steele, who scored England's goal, gave his medal to City manager Bob McGrory as a mark of gratitude. Meanwhile Stoke, without their most potent attackers, drew 0-0 at Bolton Wanderers in front of 12,000 fans.

WEDNESDAY 17TH APRIL 1996

Mike Sheron set a club record of scoring in seven consecutive league matches when he netted the only goal of the game against Charlton Athletic at the Victoria Ground. Of the seven, four were winning goals and two came in the last minute. The victory kept Stoke in fifth place and in the hunt for a play-off place.

SATURDAY 18TH APRIL 1925

A vital win against promotion-chasing Derby County kept Stoke out of the bottom two with just two games left to play. The goals at the Baseball Ground both came from Harry Davies, to leave five teams separated by one point at the foot of the table.

MONDAY 18TH APRIL 1927

Despite a goalless draw at home to Doncaster Rovers, the 15,903 crowd knew that promotion was almost assured as City were five points clear at the top of Division Three (North) with only three games remaining to be played.

SATURDAY 18TH APRIL 1998

Alan Durban was back in caretaker stewardship of the team 17 years after leaving for Sunderland. Durban's side had managed to pick up two wins in three games to lift Stoke out of the bottom three and keep alive hopes of avoiding relegation back to the third tier of English football. The 2-0 victory over Norwich City included goals for Icelander Larus Sigurdsson and Bermudan Kyle Lightbourne.

SATURDAY 19TH APRIL 1902

Hyde Road, the home of Manchester City, was the scene for a dramatic afternoon at the foot of Division One. A victory against the bottom team would see Stoke safe from relegation, but a point was all Stoke could manage thanks to an own goal from Hillman and a Tom Holford effort. The Potters had to wait for safety until the following Saturday when Small Heath could not get the win they needed to send Stoke down on goal average.

SATURDAY 19TH APRIL 1958

Aged just 16 years 153 days, Peter Bullock became the youngest player to play for the Potters first-team. In front of over 23,000 supporters, Bullock scored Stoke's goal in a 4-1 defeat to Swansea Town in the Second Division.

TUESDAY 19TH APRIL 1972

The FA Cup semi-final replay again caused heartbreak for the City fans as Stoke again led at half time, this time 1-0. Arsenal were then awarded a hotly disputed penalty by referee Walker, which Charlie George converted. The tie was over when linesman Bob Matthewson mistook a programme seller for a Stoke defender to allow Radford to run through and win it when he was offside by a distance.

SATURDAY 19TH APRIL 2008

A late kick-off due to the Sky Sports TV cameras did not put off the supporters as 24,475 turned out for the vital promotion clash against Bristol City. Mama Sidibe was the match winner for Stoke scoring twice to give his team a 2-1 win which lifted them up to second place.

SATURDAY 20TH APRIL 1889

Defeat at Accrington condemned Stoke to a bottom-place finish in the first Football League table. Stoke sought re-election – along with Notts County, Derby County and Burnley – and polled more votes, with ten, than anybody else to secure their league status.

SATURDAY 20TH APRIL 1907

A 2-0 defeat at home to Middlesbrough sent Stoke down to the Second Division for the first time ever with one match still to play.

THURSDAY 20TH APRIL 1972

Stoke City goalkeeper Gordon Banks was named Footballer of the Year for 1972 by the Football Writers, with team-mate George Eastham coming third. He became the second Potters player to be named Footballer of the Year after Stanley Matthews won the award nine years earlier in 1963. When Stan arrived to receive his award he played on his age by walking on to stage with a walking stick and a grey beard!

SATURDAY 20TH APRIL 1985

Eventual champions Everton relegated City, with seven games left to play, at the Victoria Ground with a 2-0 win: Graeme Sharp and Kevin Sheedy were on the score-sheet. A crowd of 18,258 started to cheer when Stoke made it as far as the Everton half! The match was the first under caretaker manager Tony Lacey. The former Stoke player, who appeared five times in the late 1960s, would oversee eight consecutive defeats.

MONDAY 21ST APRIL 1924

A 3-0 reverse at relegation-threatened Hull City effectively ended Stoke's promotion hopes. The season had been so promising but promotion was now only possible by goal average – unlikely with two games left.

SATURDAY 21st APRIL 1979

Stoke hit top spot in the Second Division with only two games remaining thanks to Brendan O'Callaghan's winner on the stroke of half-time. Wrexham piled on the pressure but Stoke held on to come away with the two points.

MONDAY 21st APRIL 2003

Victory at Coventry City left Stoke six points clear of Brighton & Hove Albion with only two games left. The recent run of form now stretched to only two losses in 12 games and four wins in the last six. The game was won by a Chris Iwelumo penalty which came back off the post, hit the back of keeper Montgomery on the ground, and then went into the net. In the final 20 minutes Stoke withstood intense pressure and Mark Crossley performed heroics in goal once again keeping his sixth clean sheet in nine games since signing on loan from Middlesbrough.

MONDAY 22nd APRIL 1895

With Stoke having finished their fixtures, a win for West Bromwich Albion of more than four goals in their last match would leave Stoke in the bottom three and in a relegation play-off. The Baggies beat Sheffield Wednesday 6-0 and Stoke had to face Newton Heath in a Test Match to remain in the First Division.

TUESDAY 22nd APRIL 1924

Any mathematical chance Stoke had of promotion was extinguished as Fulham took a point from the Victoria Ground. A run of only seven goals in 11 games had ultimately proved costly.

SATURDAY 22nd APRIL 1933

First Division football was all but ensured after Lincoln City were beaten 5-2 by the Potters. The enthusiastic crowd, just two short of 20,000, saw Tommy Sale grab two goals with Bobby Liddle, Harry Ware and Jack Palethorpe getting the others. Palethorpe joined Stoke for £3,000 from Reading in March 1933 specifically for the promotion push. He played in the last ten games of the season scoring an impressive eight goals.

WEDNESDAY 22ND APRIL 1964

Leicester City held out for a 3-2 victory on the night – 4-3 on aggregate – to claim the League Cup trophy. Dennis Viollet and George Kinnell scored for Stoke City who were handicapped by an injured Calvin Palmer in the second half.

SATURDAY 23RD APRIL 1892

Going into the final day of the season Stoke knew that a point would be enough to keep them off the bottom for the first time in the Football League. Joe Schofield scored the only goal of the game against West Bromwich Albion to ensure it was Darwen, and not Stoke, who finished last and were therefore the first team to be relegated to the Second Division.

SATURDAY 23RD APRIL 1904

A goal from Frank Whitehouse earned a point at home to Derby County and ensured that Liverpool rather than Stoke dropped down to Division Two. Whitehouse scored 24 goals in 95 appearances before leaving to join Glossop North End in 1905.

SATURDAY 23RD APRIL 1927

A Victoria Ground crowd of 8,440 turned out to see Stoke clinch promotion from Division Three (North) with a 1-0 victory against Accrington Stanley. The win was sealed when John Eyres kicked the ball out of the goalkeeper's hands just after half time. Defeats for both Rochdale and Nelson ensured Stoke would be back in Division Two after an absence of only one year.

SATURDAY 23RD APRIL 1960

Frank Bowyer made his final appearance for the club at the age of 38 years and 13 days. Bowyer turned professional with Stoke in 1939 and lost a large part of his career to the war, although he still went on to be one of the club's top goalscorers netting 137 league goals – second only to Freddie Steele with 140 – and 205 including cup and war matches, which has only been surpassed by Steele and Tommy Sale. He left Stoke to join Macclesfield Town.

TUESDAY 23RD APRIL 1968

With Stoke struggling just one place off the bottom of the First Division, relegation loomed with just five games to go. Don Revie's Leeds United arrived at the Victoria Ground for a thrilling match. Peter Dobing gave the home side a 2-0 half time lead with two fabulous goals, but in the second period Leeds came back with two quick-fire goals from future Stoke hero Jimmy Greenhoff, and Jack Charlton. Against the run of play, Dobing grabbed his hat-trick from a corner, and Stoke kept their survival hopes alive with some desperate defending in the last 25 minutes.

SATURDAY 24TH APRIL 1915

Stoke played their last ever non-league game against Swansea Town winning the Southern League Second Division. The match also marked the end of Peter Hodge's one season in charge of the club, before he returned to his native Scotland. In charge of only 28 league and cup matches, Hodge's record was a good one with 20 victories.

WEDNESDAY 24TH APRIL 1963

Real Madrid visited the Victoria Ground to take part in Stoke's centenary celebration match in front of 44,914 fans. Ruiz gave Real the lead early on but Stoke came back in the second half to lead through Dennis Viollet and Jimmy McIlroy. The Spanish giants, inspired by the legendary Alfredo Di Stefano, came back strongly and Ferenc Puskas equalised from the penalty spot after the great Hungarian himself was brought down, to end the match 2-2.

SATURDAY 24TH APRIL 1982

A 2-1 victory over Wolves halted the slide – no win in the previous nine – and lifted Stoke out of the relegation places. A Maguire penalty brought Stoke level and then Lee Chapman scored the winner after Andy Gray had been sent off.

SATURDAY 25TH APRIL 1903

Stoke finished the season in sixth place, the best league position so far after a 1-1 draw at Middlesbrough's Linthorpe Road Ground.

MONDAY 25TH APRIL 1910

Hastings St Leonard's provided the opposition for the Southern League Division Two Championship match in front of 3,000 spectators at the Victoria Ground. The Eastern Division winners were no match for Stoke, the Western Division winners, who won 6-0 courtesy of a William Smith hat-trick and goals from Edwin Griffiths, Harry Leese and George Turner.

SATURDAY 25TH APRIL 1953

A defeat to bottom of the table Derby County at the Victoria Ground left Stoke in a precarious position. Frank Bowyer's goal, only his third of the season, was not enough in front of the near 30,000 crowd, and Derby took the points winning 2-1. With all of their games completed, Stoke were only one point above Chelsea who had a game left to play.

MONDAY 25TH APRIL 1955

Stoke went to the top of the Second Division with one game remaining after beating Port Vale 1-0 at Vale Park, although other clubs had games in hand. A Bowyer goal settled the game in front of 40,066, which was a record home league gate for the Burslem club.

WEDNESDAY 25TH APRIL 1979

A nervous Stoke side failed to find a way through Newcastle United's defence and had to settle for a goalless draw in front of 23,271 at the Victoria Ground. Alan Durban's Potters now had to wait until the last game of the season against Notts County at Meadow Lane to try and claim promotion back to the First Division.

SATURDAY 25TH APRIL 1992

Relegation strugglers Chester City came to Stoke and shattered any automatic promotion hopes for the Potters. City now had to rely on Brentford dropping points in their games in hand to stand any chance. It looked like a first modern play-off experience for Lou Macari and his team after they had been top of the table with just four games to go, and second prior to this match.

SATURDAY 26TH APRIL 1952

After overcoming a terrible start to the 1951/52 season, Stoke found themselves back in the bottom two after winning only three out of eighteen matches. A 3-1 victory at home to Manchester City in front of a 25,000 strong crowd lifted them out of trouble. Brian Siddall, Sammy Smyth and Frank Bowyer were the heroes, but it was time for a change of manager and Bob McGrory would soon be replaced by Frank Taylor.

SATURDAY 26TH APRIL 1975

Stoke were unable to beat Burnley in the last match of the season and so the season petered out to nothing. City had taken only two points from the last three matches which left them just four points adrift of champions Derby County in fifth place. They did not even claim a Uefa Cup place as the rules regarding 'one club, one city' were changed and Everton qualified.

SATURDAY 26TH APRIL 2003

Needing a point to ensure survival, Stoke were nearly safe until Dele Adebola scored in the 82nd minute for Crystal Palace at Selhurst Park. Brighton & Hove Albion beat Watford 4-0 to take the relegation battle to the last match with City needing only a point to be safe.

SATURDAY 26TH APRIL 2008

The last game at Colchester United's Layer Road finished with a 1-0 victory for the Potters. Richard Cresswell's close-range effort moved City to within one point of the Premiership.

SATURDAY 27TH APRIL 1895

Having finished third from bottom of the First Division, Stoke had to play Newton Heath, who finished third in the Second Division, in a Test Match for a place in the top flight. The game, played at Port Vale's Cobridge Athletic Ground, finished 3-0 to Stoke thanks to two goals from Joe Schofield and one from John Farrell. The Potters maintained their place in the First Division, but despite the victory this was Arthur Reeves last game as manager.

SATURDAY 27TH APRIL 1908

Defeat at home to Leicester Fosse, by the only goal of the game, left Stoke tenth in the Second Division at the end of the season. During the summer Stoke resigned from the league and it would be another 11 years until league football returned to the Victoria Ground. The collapse of the club saw the end of Horace Denham Austerberry's time as manager. 'Denny' had been in charge for 11 years and was noted as a strict disciplinarian. On one occasion he is reputed to have suspended three of the Stoke players because they had been drinking champagne! Under Austerberry's stewardship Stoke won 136 and lost 172 of his 386 league games in charge.

THURSDAY 27TH APRIL 1911

The Potters' 5-1 win at Kettering Town clinched promotion and the runners-up spot in the Southern League Division Two, behind champions Reading on goal average and two points ahead of Merthyr Tydfil.

MONDAY 27TH APRIL 1925

A defeat in the last game of the season at Chelsea left Stoke ahead of Oldham Athletic on goal average and one point above Crystal Palace, who had still to play each other. Knowing a draw would relegate Stoke, it was a relief that the match was competitive as Oldham came away from London with a 1-0 victory and Stoke were safe in the Second Division for another year.

WEDNESDAY 28TH APRIL 1919

Some 46 years before the formal introduction of substitutes, Charlie Parker was replaced by E.F. Turner in the wartime fixture against Port Vale. There were 16,000 at the Old Recreation Ground for the match which Vale won 4-1, with Billy Herbert scoring Stoke's consolation.

SATURDAY 28TH APRIL 1923

A goalless draw at home to Liverpool, who had already been crowned champions, was not enough for Stoke to stay up and they were relegated back to the Second Division after only one season.

WEDNESDAY 28TH APRIL 1965

Sir Stanley Matthews took to the field for the last time in a Stoke City shirt for his testimonial at the Victoria Ground in front of a packed 35,000 crowd. The match attracted global media interest as a Stanley Matthews XI took on a World XI, with an estimated audience of 112 million tuning in. Many of the greatest names in the game turned out to honour the 'Wizard of the Dribble'. At the end of the match, 33 years after making his debut, 50-year-old Matthews was carried from the field on the shoulders of Lev Yashin and Ferenc Puskas, after inspiring his side to a thrilling 6-4 victory.

SATURDAY 28TH APRIL 1990

With relegation already confirmed, the last away game of the season at Brighton & Hove Albion's Goldstone Ground was advertised as a beach party. A large and colourful away following turned up in fancy dress and good spirits to witness an out-of-character display from Stoke as they ran out 4-1 winners, the first win in 21 games.

WEDNESDAY 28TH APRIL 1993

Nigel Gleghorn scored, after only four minutes, past former Stoke goalkeeper Peter Shilton to clinch promotion and the Second Division title for the Potters. Plymouth battled gamely and forced Peter Fox into an outstanding double save, but Stoke held on. Wild celebrations followed as Stoke's three-year exile in the third tier was over.

SUNDAY 28TH APRIL 2002

A strong second-half comeback from Stoke was not enough to prevent Cardiff City from taking a goal advantage back to Ninian Park for the second leg of the play-off semi-final. Deon Burton, on loan from Derby County, reduced the arrears to 2-1 to give some hope for the return.

SATURDAY 29TH APRIL 1911

As well as gaining promotion in the Southern League, Stoke claimed the Birmingham and District League title after a 3-2 victory at Brierley Hill Alliance.

SATURDAY 29TH APRIL 1922

A 2-0 defeat at the hands of Bristol City saw Stoke drop out of the top two in the Second Division with only one game to go. The Ashton Gate defeat came during a run of only two points gained from five games played.

WEDNESDAY 29TH APRIL 1953

Without kicking a ball, Frank Taylor's Stoke City were relegated back to the Second Division after 20 years in the top flight. Chelsea earned a 3-1 victory against Manchester City at Stamford Bridge to leapfrog City to First Division safety. Stoke were relegated by a single point.

SATURDAY 29TH APRIL 1961

A 2-0 defeat against Brighton & Hove Albion in front of only 5,232 home fans left Stoke with only one win in the last nine matches, and perilously close to dropping to the Third Division for only the second time in their history. The game saw the debut of Gerry Bridgewood, aged only 16 years and 194 days, who became the second youngest player to represent Stoke.

MONDAY 29TH APRIL 1974

Stoke claimed a Uefa Cup spot with a 1-0 victory over Manchester United that stretched their unbeaten run to nine games and lifted them to fifth in the table. The victory was sealed by 'Big John' Ritchie with a goal on the half hour, but the star turn was Alan Hudson who ran rings around the opposition. United were already relegated and their fans ran riot and set fire to banners.

SATURDAY 30TH APRIL 1898

Stoke, Blackburn Rovers, Burnley and Newcastle United were involved in an end-of-season Test Match competition for two places in the top division. The final match between Stoke and Burnley was a dour 0-0 draw as both sides only needed a point in the mini-league. There was not much attacking football and at one point the 15,000-strong crowd kept the ball to try and keep themselves amused!

SATURDAY 30TH APRIL 1921

A poor performance at Ashton Gate saw Bristol City run out 5-0 winners. Stoke had now not won in nine games and dropped to two places above the bottom spot. Fortunately, Stockport County had been so poor they could not catch anyone and were already doomed to the Third Division.

THURSDAY 30TH APRIL 1931

The final home game of the season doubled as Bobby Archibald's benefit game, and a crowd of 26,064 turned out to see Stoke City beaten 1-0 by West Bromwich Albion. Archibald was an outside-left signed from Third Lanark in 1925 as a 30-year-old. Nicknamed 'Steve' due to his resemblance to jockey Steve Donoghue, he scored 40 goals in 276 appearances.

SATURDAY 30TH APRIL 1955

Stoke conspired to miss out on promotion by dropping out of the top two after the last match of the season. Plymouth's 2-0 victory denied City any hope of promotion although Birmingham City won their game in hand so the Potters would have missed out on goal average anyway even if they had won.

SATURDAY 30TH APRIL 1960

The 1959/60 season petered out with a 2-1 win at Bristol City thanks to Johnny King and an own goal from Williams in front of only 8,722. Disenchantment gripped the Stoke faithful as crowds reached their lowest levels for decades and a return to the First Division seemed as far away as it had ever been. With this backdrop, the board decided not to renew the contract of manager Frank Taylor after eight years in charge, a decision which paved the way for assistant manager Tony Waddington to take over after initially joining the club in 1952.

SUNDAY 30TH APRIL 2006

The end of Johan Boskamp's tenure as manager saw the Potters face Brighton & Hove Albion at their temporary Withdean Stadium home. Stoke ran riot and young Irish striker Adam Rooney became the youngest Stoke player to score a hat-trick, aged 18 years and nine days. Mama Sidibe and Peter Sweeney also scored as City romped home 5-1.

SATURDAY 1st MAY 1926

After two successive victories, Stoke went into the last match of the season behind Clapton Orient on goal average and one point behind Fulham, but with a vastly superior goal average. Dick Johnson scored his 13th goal of the season as Stoke drew 1-1 at home to Southampton. However, it was unlucky for some as Fulham beat Bradford City 2-0 at Craven Cottage and Orient beat Middlesbrough 2-1 at Ayresome Park. Stoke dropped into the Third Division for the very first time by just a single point.

WEDNESDAY 1st MAY 1968

Stoke beat bottom-of-the-table Fulham at Craven Cottage to lift themselves out of the relegation places with three matches to go, and relegated their hosts to the Second Division in the process. The vital 2-0 victory saw goals from Roy Vernon and Peter Dobing.

WEDNESDAY 1st MAY 2002

A remarkable late fight back from the Potters meant a place in the play-off final at the Millennium Stadium. Cardiff City were already planning their victory parade when James O'Connor scored through ex-Potter Graham Kavanagh's legs in the last minute to level things up 2-2 on aggregate and force extra time. The drama was completed in the second period of extra time as O'Connor's free-kick deflected in off Souleymane Oulare's backside and Stoke were in the final, ironically at the Millennium Stadium – in Cardiff!

SATURDAY 2nd MAY 1936

Liverpool were beaten 2-1 at the Victoria Ground thanks to a Bradshaw own goal and a Jim Westland strike. The win meant Stoke finished the season in fourth place, their best ever league finish.

WEDNESDAY 2nd MAY 1973

Wing-half Willie Stevenson was released by Stoke after six years service and over 100 games. Signed from Liverpool for £48,000, he moved to Tranmere Rovers after his final year in the Potteries was shattered due to a broken leg. He scored 7 goals for the Potters.

SATURDAY 2ND MAY 1981

Paul Bracewell scored his first goals in the league, against Wolves, to finish the season on a high with a 3-2 win at the Victoria Ground. The game turned out to be Alan Durban's last as manager, as he left in the summer to take up a post at Sunderland saying he wanted to manage a 'big club'.

SATURDAY 2ND MAY 1992

Defeat at Bolton Wanderers ensured Stoke reached the play-offs, which was a bit of disappointment having led the table for so long. Mark Stein gave Lou Macari's side the lead at half-time but Bolton scored three after the break to claim all three points.

SATURDAY 3RD MAY 1930

The last game of the season against Tottenham Hotspur doubled as a testimonial match for Len Armitage. A poor crowd of just 6,570 turned out to see City win 1-0 thanks to Jack Cull. Armitage, who had signed from Wigan Borough in 1923, was a centre-forward who didn't have the best goalscoring record; he only netted 19 times in 200 games for Stoke.

SATURDAY 3RD MAY 1947

Freddie Steele scored his 30th and 31st goals of the season to beat Leeds United 2-1 at Elland Road. The run of seven consecutive victories had left Stoke just a point behind leaders Wolves with just three games remaining and gave them a real chance of the title.

SATURDAY 3RD MAY 1952

Roy Brown chalked up two goals as Stoke beat Middlesbrough 3-2 on the last day of the season. The other goal for the Potters was a collectors' item as John McCue scored one of only two goals in his league career in 502 Football League appearances. The game marked the end of Bob McGrory's long association with the club as he stepped down as manager aged 61. The dour Scotsman had joined the club in 1921 from Burnley as a full-back.

WEDNESDAY 3RD MAY 1961

Stoke beat Liverpool 3-1 at the Victoria Ground in the last game of the season. The match had originally been played in early December but was abandoned at half-time when it was still goalless. In the rematch Bill Bentley scored twice and Johnny King grabbed one.

SUNDAY 3RD MAY 1998

A sell-out crowd of 26,664 turned up at the Britannia Stadium for the relegation dogfight with Manchester City. Stoke capitulated and lost 5-2, despite two goals from Peter Thorne, as fighting broke out amongst the fans. Port Vale won 4-0 at Huddersfield to relegate both Stoke and Manchester City to the Second Division. This would be Stoke's third spell in the third tier of English football.

SUNDAY 4TH MAY 1918

As winners of the Lancashire Section of the wartime league, Stoke faced Leeds City, who were the Midlands Section champions, in a two-legged final known as the League Championship Cup. The first leg at Leeds did not go well and Stoke lost 2-0 in front of 15,000.

SATURDAY 4TH MAY 1935

Bob McGrory, who had already retired once, became the oldest player to be ever-present in the First Division at 42-years-old. Stoke's 2-0 victory over Huddersfield Town, thanks to goals from Harry Davies and an Arthur Turner penalty, also marked the last match with Tom Mather as manager before McGrory himself took over the reins.

SUNDAY 4TH MAY 1997

The oldest league ground in the world played host to its last competitive match against West Bromwich Albion. The Victoria Ground was packed to its reduced capacity of 22,500 to see Stoke beat the Baggies 2-1 thanks to Gerry McMahon and Graham Kavanagh. The largest terrace left in England – The Boothen End – finally said goodbye after 119 years. It was also a second farewell from popular manager Lou Macari as he departed to fight a court case against his previous employers Celtic.

SUNDAY 4th MAY 2003

It was a tense afternoon as Stoke needed only a point against Reading to be safe and avoid returning to the Second Division at the first time of asking. Ade Akinbiyi scored early in the second half to trigger delirium amongst the 20,477 present as safety was secured and the Brighton & Hove Albion score no longer mattered. The turnaround from mid-February had been astonishing and Tony Pulis had pulled off a miracle.

SUNDAY 4th MAY 2008

A dramatic final day of the season saw Stoke draw 0-0 with Leicester City to ensure a long-awaited promotion to the Premiership, whilst the Foxes were relegated to League One for the first time in their history. Tony Pulis' Potters knew before kick-off that a point would be sufficient to send them up. However, the 26,609 fans were nervous throughout the tense afternoon. Ricardo Fuller had a couple of chances to give City the lead, but as goals were going in elsewhere it was Leicester who became increasingly dominant. It took a couple of fine saves from on-loan Carlo Nash to keep Stoke level before news filtered through that Hull City were losing. City could celebrate! The final whistle signalled an enormous pitch invasion as the fans realised the 23-year wait for a return to the top flight was over.

SATURDAY 5th MAY 1945

Just days before VE Day a mere 800 turned out to see the local derby against Port Vale. The few who did attend saw Stoke emerge victorious as they scored six goals without reply, with George Mountford hitting four.

SATURDAY 5th MAY 1979

Home fans are outnumbered at Meadow Lane as Stoke aimed for promotion. Nerves were frayed but Paul Richardson scored at the death to earn a place back in the First Division. Sunderland lost out as Alan Durban's Potters finished third behind Crystal Palace and Brighton & Hove Albion.

SUNDAY 5TH MAY 1996

A 12th-minute Mike Sheron rocket secured a play-off spot for Stoke in a nervous encounter against Southend United at the Victoria Ground. The pitch invasion by the majority of the 18,897 crowd caused the referee to blow his final whistle three minutes early. This was Stoke's first opportunity to return to the top flight via the play-offs and they would face Leicester City.

SATURDAY 5TH MAY 2001

Swindon Town were beaten 4-1 at the Britannia Stadium as Stoke sealed a play-off berth for the second successive year. Goals from Brynjar Gunnarsson, Graham Kavanagh, Andy Cooke and a Keith O'Halloran own goal won it in front of 20,591 fans.

SATURDAY 6TH MAY 1922

Stoke played their last game of the season after Barnsley had already finished their fixtures, so the Potters knew that only a victory was good enough for promotion. Two goals from Arty Watkin, and one from Fred Groves, saw Stoke beat Bristol City 3-0 and secure promotion back to Division One on goal average, and relegate Bristol. Watkin scored his two goals despite playing with a splintered ankle.

SATURDAY 6TH MAY 1933

The Second Division title was clinched with a 4-1 victory over Bradford City at the Victoria Ground in front of 17,380. Stoke had already sealed a return to the top flight of English football after an absence of ten years. The trophy was claimed by finishing one point ahead of Tottenham Hotspur after two goals by Bobby Liddle and one each for Tommy Sale and Arthur Turner. It would be another 20 years before the Potters slipped back into the Second Division.

SATURDAY 6TH MAY 2000

Reading beat Stoke 1-0 at their new Madejski Stadium but the Potters still secured a play-off spot to face Gillingham thanks to Bristol Rovers' 1-0 defeat at Cardiff City. Former Spurs man Darren Caskey scored Reading's winner with an 81st-minute penalty.

SUNDAY 6TH MAY 2007

Queens Park Rangers held Stoke to a draw and denied the Potters a play-off spot. The disappointment was felt just as keenly at the Britannia Stadium as the club had laid on a live beam-back of the match to a large screen at the ground, which would be repeated 12 months later.

SATURDAY 7TH MAY 1927

Stoke said goodbye to the Third Division (North) in style by thrashing Halifax Town in the last game of the season. The goals were shared by Harry Davies and Jack Eyres – two each – while Bobby Archibald claimed the other. The last five games of the season had yielded four wins and a draw to leave Stoke five points clear with a fantastic goal average of 2.30. On winning the title, Charlie Wilson became the first person to complete a hat-trick of medals having won the First, Second and now Third divisions.

SATURDAY 7TH MAY 1938

Freddie Steele had a day to remember as he scored the second goal in a 2-0 win against Liverpool – Frank Baker scored the first – which ensured survival in the First Division. Steele had married in secret on the morning of the match with the only player in the know being captain Arthur Turner who gave the bride away!

FRIDAY 7TH MAY 1971

At Selhurst Park only 5,031 turned up on the eve of the cup final to see Stoke take on Everton in the FA Cup third-place play-off match. Stoke ran out 3-2 winners after going 2-0 down early on. The victory was secured by two goals from John Ritchie and one from Mike Bernard.

MONDAY 7TH MAY 1973

Liverpool reserves shared a goalless draw with their Bury counterparts at Gigg Lane to push Stoke reserves down into runners-up spot in the Central League. Stoke City reserves have twice won the Central League: in 1927/28 and 1991/92.

MONDAY 7TH MAY 1984

A run of poor form – no win in four – came to an end with a victory at Luton Town thanks to an Ian Painter goal after five minutes. This meant Stoke could stay up with a victory over Wolves, already down.

MONDAY 8TH MAY 1950

Risking suspension for leaving the boundaries of Fifa, George Mountford and Neil Franklin headed to Colombia to play for Independiente Santa Fe. Their departure, with other players such as Charlie Mitten, caused a media sensation, particularly with Franklin as Walter Winterbottom wanted him to play in the World Cup Finals in Brazil. Franklin returned to England within two months but would never play for England or City again, whilst Mountford completed the season before returning to Stoke after suspension.

SATURDAY 8TH MAY 1993

The Second Division trophy was presented to Stoke captain Vince Overson before the match against Burnley at the Victoria Ground. The game was almost incidental and finished 1-1, with Mark Stein scoring his 33rd goal of the season, and Peter Fox saying goodbye after 15 years' service with Stoke.

SATURDAY 8TH MAY 1999

Brian Little fielded a young team for what would turn out to be his last match in charge. It worked as Stoke notched only their second win in nine thanks to a brace from Paul Connor. A season which had started out so brightly by winning the first six matches and still being top in December, had fizzled out to nothing. Over the summer Little left the club.

SUNDAY 8TH MAY 2005

Manager Tony Pulis and the fans had little idea that the Welshman's first spell in charge of the club was about to come to an end. The last game of the season was a tricky trip to champions Sunderland at the Stadium of Light. Stoke fought well but the Black Cats were too strong and won 1-0.

SATURDAY 9TH MAY 1942

Frankie Soo became the first non-white player to earn an England cap when he turned out in the 1-0 defeat to Wales at Ninian Park in front of 30,000. The game was won by a first-half William Lucas goal.

SATURDAY 9TH MAY 1987

During the 1986/87 season, Stoke City played Grimsby Town a total of five times and the results sequence was: 1-1, 1-1, 1-1, 6-0 and 5-2. The final day victory in front of a disappointing 6,406 came with five different goalscorers – Tony Kelly, Brian Talbot, George Berry, Carl Saunders and Tony Ford.

SATURDAY 9TH MAY 2004

A goalless draw on the last day of the season was enough to ensure visitors Gillingham's survival. A crowd of 19,240 came in the hope of seeing some drama, but went away disappointed.

SATURDAY 10TH MAY 1947

Stanley Matthews was sold to Blackpool for £11,500 after he had again asked for a transfer. Stoke had sold their best player, with only three games left, whilst sitting in second place and within reach of their first league title! The money was less than it could have been because everyone thought Stan was towards the end of his career aged 32. He carried on playing for another 18 years!

SUNDAY 10TH MAY 1964

On a tour organised by Charlie Mitten, who went to Colombia with Neil Franklin in 1950, Stoke lost to Sante Fe; the club Franklin and George Mountford played for. The team from Bogota beat the Potters 3-2 after Stoke were 2-0 up at half-time. Goals from Calvin Palmer and Peter Dobing came before Stoke ran out of steam due to an altitude of over 8,000 feet.

SUNDAY 10TH MAY 1992

Carl Beeston was sent off in the play-off semi-final first leg for a bad challenge at Edgeley Park. Stoke were swiftly made to pay as Stockport County took a 1-0 advantage into the second leg.

MONDAY 10TH MAY 1993

For ten minutes during Gordon Cowans' testimonial at Villa Park, Stoke were officially allowed to play with 12 men! Neil Baldwin, the rotund kit man, also known as 'Nello the Clown', came onto the pitch to take part in the match. With the Villa defence parting and Nigel Spink getting into the spirit and playing scared, Nello lined up a shot only for Tony Kelly to take the ball from his foot and fire it over the bar! At the end of the match Nello tried to swap shirts with David Platt.

SATURDAY 11TH MAY 1918

The second leg of the League Championship Final saw Stoke beat Leeds City 1-0 in front of 14,500 supporters. A penalty from Charlie Parker was not enough to overturn the 2-0 first leg deficit and Leeds won on aggregate. Next season Stoke just missed out on another appearance in the final after finishing second in the Lancashire Section to Everton.

WEDNESDAY 11TH MAY 1977

Garth Crooks earned a point for Stoke against Manchester United as City came from behind to draw 3-3. The point left the Potters just three points above the relegation places with other teams having games in hand.

SATURDAY 11TH MAY 2002

Cardiff's Millennium Stadium was the venue for the play-off final which saw Stoke promoted back to the second tier of English football after a four-year wait. Gudjon Thordarsson's men rarely looked troubled against Brentford and ran out 2-0 winners in front of 42,523 fans, most of whom were from the Potteries. The vital goals came from Deon Burton and an own goal from Brentford's Ben Burgess. It was fifth time lucky for Stoke in the modern-era play-offs and Peter Handyside collected the trophy. Bizarrely, this turned out to be Thordarsson's last game in charge before being sacked by his fellow Icelanders in the boardroom, headed by chairman Gunnar Thor Gislason.

SATURDAY 12TH MAY 1984

Stoke needed to beat already relegated Wolves by as many as possible to avoid joining their opponents in the Second Division. The Potters won convincingly 4-0 with all of the goals scored by Paul Maguire, the first Stoke player to score four in a match for 18 years. It was rumoured that former City stalwart Alan Dodd, now playing for Wolves, deliberately gave Stoke a penalty – one of two that day – to help his beloved club stay up! The win was just enough as only one of Stoke's four relegation rivals, Birmingham City, failed to win their final match. The Potters were safe – for now!

SUNDAY 12TH MAY 1996

Leicester City clung on at Filbert Street for a 0-0 draw as Stoke pressed hard for a goal in the First Division play-off semi-final first leg. Somehow, City failed to capitalise on a below par Foxes performance with Kevin Poole making some great saves, particularly from Simon Sturridge and Graham Potter when it seemed easier to score.

WEDNESDAY 13TH MAY 1992

A first-minute goal from Chris Beaumont gave Stoke a mountain to climb at 2-0 down on aggregate in front of a home crowd of 16,170. Stockport County hung on, despite a late Mark Stein strike, to earn a place in the Third Division play-off final.

SATURDAY 13TH MAY 2000

Stoke took the lead in the play-off semi-final against Gillingham through Arnar Gunnlaugsson after just 25 seconds at the Britannia Stadium. Further goals from Kyle Lightbourne and Peter Thorne should have made things comfortable in the second leg, but a screamer from Andy Hessenthaler deep into injury time kept the tie alive.

SUNDAY 13TH MAY 2001

The first leg of the Second Division play-off semi-final with Walsall ended 0-0 in front of 23,689. Stoke were now second favourites to progress as they went to the second leg at the Bescot Stadium.

TUESDAY 14TH MAY 1963

Thousands of Stokies journeyed to Gigg Lane expecting to see the club clinch a return to the First Division after a ten-year absence. The game did not go to plan and Stoke, without Stanley Matthews, lost 2-1 despite a Jackie Mudie goal. The promotion celebration would have to wait. This was Mudie's best goalscoring season with Stoke as he netted 20 league goals, just behind leading scorer Dennis Viollet with 23. This was the first and last time that Stoke had two players who reached 20 league goals in a single season.

THURSDAY 14TH MAY 1964

Colombian side Medellin provided the opposition for the next match on Stoke's South American tour. John Ritchie, Peter Dobing and Dennis Viollet scored the goals in a 3-0 win.

TUESDAY 14TH MAY 1985

West Ham United secured their place in the top flight with a 5-1 victory as Stoke dropped out of Division One with little dignity remaining. Ian Painter scored City's last goal in the First Division from the penalty spot to finish as top scorer with six goals, although only two of those were from open play.

WEDNESDAY 15TH MAY 1968

Third-placed Liverpool visited Stoke for the final game of the season with City languishing in 20th place, although safe from relegation. A fine performance by the Potters resulted in a 2-1 win thanks to goals from Peter Dobing and John Mahoney to ensure a final position of 18th.

THURSDAY 15TH MAY 1969

European Cup Winners' Cup holders Barcelona hosted Stoke for a friendly match in front of around 65,000 people in the impressive Camp Nou. Two goals from David Herd and one from Harry Burrows gave the Potters a 3-0 half-time lead, and despite a strong second-half fight back from Barça, Stoke held out to win 3-2 against their Spanish hosts.

SATURDAY 15TH MAY 1982

Norman Whiteside scored on his debut for Manchester United, along with Bryan Robson, to help beat Stoke 2-0 and ensure that City had to beat fellow strugglers West Bromwich Albion in their last game of the season to stay in the division.

WEDNESDAY 15TH MAY 1996

A superb finish from Garry Parker gave Leicester City a place in the First Division play-off final, and ultimately the Premiership. Most of the 21,037 crowd were distraught. City were dominant in the first leg and the supporters truly believed this was Stoke's year to go up. Stoke had beaten the Foxes both home and away during the normal fixtures.

MONDAY 16TH MAY 1977

Stoke completed the slide into the Second Division for the first time since 1963 as an Andy Gray penalty was enough for Aston Villa to take two points at Villa Park. West Ham United survived after beating Manchester United 4-2, but Stoke's downfall was spectacular. On 23rd April they were 15th, but five games later they had fallen six places and were down and relegated after 14 years in the top flight.

SATURDAY 16TH MAY 1992

Mark Stein scored the only goal of the game at Wembley in front of 48,339 spectators. The majority were Stoke fans who saw captain Vince Overson lift the Autoglass Trophy. The result was sweet revenge for the Stoke faithful who had just three days earlier seen their opponents Stockport County beat them in the play-off semi-final to reach Wembley again.

WEDNESDAY 16TH MAY 2001

Stoke capitulated 4-2 to Walsall in the play-off semi-final second leg, despite taking the lead through Graham Kavanagh. The fans were baffled by Gudjon Thordarson's decision to leave top scorer Peter Thorne on the bench and play just one striker up front. Thorne came off the bench to score Stoke's second. However, Walsall had scored four in the meantime to win the tie.

THURSDAY 16TH MAY 2002

Despite winning promotion, Gudjon Thordarson was sacked by his Icelandic compatriots just five days after winning the play-off final.

SATURDAY 17TH MAY 1947

Stoke, having incredibly just sold their best player whilst only one point away from the top of the table, could only play out a goalless draw in their final home game against Sunderland. Although this did not rule out the league title it meant that any slip up would be costly.

FRIDAY 17TH MAY 1985

Stoke took almost all of the worst-ever records as they dropped out of the First Division with a 1-0 defeat at home to Coventry City. It would be 23 years until top-flight football returned to Stoke.

WEDNESDAY 17TH MAY 2000

Referee Rob Styles was the main talking point for sending off two Stoke players with the score at 0-0 in the second leg of the play-off semi-final. With Clive Clarke and Graham Kavanagh off the field, Gillingham started to press and got the goal they needed after 55 minutes to force extra time. Iffy Onuora and Paul Smith capitalised on Stoke's tiredness in the extra period to send the Gills to Wembley.

SATURDAY 18TH MAY 1963

A joyous pitch invasion at the final whistle signalled the end of Stoke's ten-year exile from the First Division. Jackie Mudie had given City the lead against visitors Luton Town, but the fairytale became reality for most of the 33,000 crowd as Stanley Matthews rounded Ron Baynham to score the second and clinch promotion.

FRIDAY 18TH MAY 1973

On the end of season tour to Australia and New Zealand, Stoke took on a combined Otago-Southland team in Dunedin and beat them 8-1 with all eight goals being scored by John Ritchie. With John Farmer in goal for the Potters, Gordon Banks played the second half for the hosts, but it made no difference as they conceded four in each half.

SATURDAY 18TH MAY 1974

The short international career of Mike Pejic came to an end. Pejic earned his fourth and final England cap against Scotland at Wembley.

THURSDAY 19TH MAY 1994

John Malkin, who took over as outside-right from Stanley Matthews on his departure to Blackpool, died in his hometown of Stoke-on-Trent. After playing 190 times in his ten years at City, his only club, he was granted a joint testimonial with George Bourne. Stoke-born full-back Bourne played 109 times for the Potters between 1951 and 1955 before a broken leg ended his career at 24-years-old.

TUESDAY 20TH MAY 1975

With almost the perfect name to play for Stoke City, Graham Potter was born in Solihull. His short career with the club totalled 58 appearances before he moved to Premier League Southampton for £250,000 in 1996.

THURSDAY 20TH MAY 1982

Stoke went into the last match of the season knowing they must win to stay in the First Division and instead relegate Leeds United, whose manager Allan Clarke was present to see the visit of West Bromwich Albion. Goals from Dave Watson, Lee Chapman and Brendan O'Callaghan gave Stoke a 3-0 victory and meant they were safe and Leeds were down. The match also marked the end of Denis Smith's Stoke City career. Smith's significant contribution to the Potters was: 14 years, 488 appearances, 42 goals, five broken legs, four broken noses, a broken ankle, a broken collar bone, a chipped spine, a ricked back, over 100 facial stitches, many broken fingers, and one reading of the last rites after picking up a serious injury on the pitch!

SUNDAY 21ST MAY 1905

At Monk Bretton in Yorkshire, future Stoke City full-back Arthur Beachill was born. He played nearly 140 games for the club before leaving for Millwall in 1934. Beachill tragically died of a heart attack returning from his work at a munitions factory in Stoke in 1943.

THURSDAY 21st MAY 1964

A crowd of around 80,000 saw a 0-0 draw as Stoke's South American tour brought them to Universidadi in Santiago, Chile.

WEDNESDAY 22nd MAY 1946

Howard Kendall was born in Ryton-on-Tyne and went on to enjoy a long career in the game. He made his name as a player, and a manager, with Everton, but between these two spells with the Toffees he was associated with Birmingham City, Blackburn Rovers and Stoke City. He made 91 appearances, scoring ten goals, all in the Second Division between 1977 and 1979, whilst player-coach for the Potters.

WEDNESDAY 22nd MAY 1963

Despite being crowned as champions just four days earlier, Stoke City's season ended with a 2-0 defeat to Southampton at The Dell.

TUESDAY 22nd MAY 1979

Brendan O'Callaghan made his international debut for the Republic of Ireland against West Germany in Dublin. His appearance, coming on as a 15th-minute substitute for Don Givens, meant Stoke had to pay an extra £5,000 to his previous club Doncaster Rovers.

SATURDAY 23rd MAY 1942

Northampton Town become only the second club to inflict a double figure defeat on Stoke with a 10-0 thumping at the County Ground. The war provided many high scoring matches.

SUNDAY 23rd MAY 1954

Bob McGrory died in Glasgow aged 62. McGrory joined Stoke from Burnley in 1921 and, despite not "liking the look of the place", he went on to serve the club for the next 31 years as both player and manager. The right-back made a total of 511 appearances before taking over the managerial reins from Tom Mather in 1935. He eventually left the club in 1952, after guiding them close to the league title in 1947 – and to its highest placed finish – and will be forever remembered as the man who fell out with Stanley Matthews and sold him to Blackpool.

TUESDAY 23RD MAY 2006

The Icelandic reign at the Britannia Stadium came to an end as Peter Coates purchased the club back. The deal involved £1.7m to buy out the shareholders, Stoke Holding SA, and £8.3m to stabilise the club's finances. The six-year Icelandic ownership had brought a trophy, two years of play-off heartache, a play-off success, steadying of the ship under Tony Pulis and a last tilt at promotion with Johan Boskamp.

SUNDAY 24TH MAY 1964

The only real disaster of City's trip to South America saw them lose 5-0 to Argentinian giants Club Atlético River Plate in Buenos Aires – where John Ritchie was sent off – at the El Monumental stadium. The next match was with River Plate's Superclásico rivals, Boca Juniors.

SATURDAY 24TH MAY 2008

Stoke City midfielder Glenn Whelan made his debut for Giovanni Trappatoni's Republic of Ireland side in a 1-1 draw against Serbia.

SATURDAY 25TH MAY 1940

Syd Peppit scored the decisive goal as Stoke ran out 3-2 winners against Manchester United at the Victoria Ground. The result ensured them the War League Western Division Championship in the first season of war football, although there were only 3,227 there to see it.

TUESDAY 25TH MAY 1971

Paolo Pasquale Peschisolido, also known as Paul, was born in Ontario in Canada. The small and nimble forward cost Stoke £400,000 from Birmingham City and was sold to rivals West Bromwich Albion two years later for £600,000, having scored 24 goals in 81 games.

MONDAY 26TH MAY 1947

George Mountford scored the winning goal at Aston Villa to ensure the title was in Stoke's hands. The victory in front of 42,000 fans left Stoke unbeaten in 11, including eight victories. Two points from the final game at Bramall Lane would see Stoke crowned as Football League champions. The wait was nearly three weeks for the match.

TUESDAY 26TH MAY 1964

The second game in Buenos Aires, against Boca Juniors, was a much closer affair than the first fixture against River Plate. Stoke beat 'Los Xeneizes' 2-1 in the Estadio Camilo Cichero, thanks to goals from Jimmy McIlroy and Tony Allen.

FRIDAY 26TH MAY 1967

Stoke had entered the United Soccer Association – forebear of the NASL – as the Cleveland Stokers and started their campaign beating Scottish side Aberdeen 2-1 thanks to goals from Maurice Setters and Roy Vernon. Aberdeen were playing in the tournament as the Washington Whips, one of 12 overseas teams in the competition.

WEDNESDAY 26TH MAY 1971

The first competitive match Stoke had ever played against a European side ended in a 2-2 draw at the Victoria Ground. AS Roma were the visitors for a bad-tempered Anglo-Italian Cup game in which there were six bookings and Mike Bernard was sent off for an alleged elbow. The City goals came from Jimmy Greenhoff and Denis Smith. Shrewsbury-born midfielder Bernard played 177 times for Stoke, winning a League Cup winners medal, before moving to Everton for £140,000 shortly after the Wembley final. He later played for Oldham Athletic before retiring through injury in May 1979.

MONDAY 27TH MAY 1929

Bobby Cairns, who played 196 times for Stoke at wing-half, was born in Glenboig near to Glasgow. He joined City from Ayr United in 1953 and stayed for eight years before moving to Macclesfield Town after a knee injury hampered his Stoke career. Cairns also played for the now defunct Third Lanark prior to joining Ayr United.

SATURDAY 27TH MAY 1950

Stoke forward Frank Bowyer appeared for the FA XI on tour in North America. He scored four as the tourists beat Saskatoon All-Stars 19-1. The FA XI, which included Stanley Matthews, played a total of 11 games on the tour and won them all, scoring 74 and conceding 14.

A STATUE OF STANLEY MATTHEWS, WHO FEATURED ON THE FA'S TOUR OF NORTH AMERICA IN MAY 1950

SATURDAY 27TH MAY 1972

Gordon Banks won the last of his 73 England caps – 36 while at Stoke, which is a record for the club – in a 1-0 victory over Scotland in Glasgow. His international career lasted nine years from April 1963.

MONDAY 27TH MAY 2002

Up-and-coming young boss Steve Cotterill was appointed as Gudjon Thordarson's successor. Cotterill had led Cheltenham Town from the Southern League, in the depths of the non-league pyramid, to the Second Division of the Football League in just five years in charge.

MONDAY 28TH MAY 1979

Blackburn Rovers were being linked with Stoke's midfielder Howard Kendall for their vacant manager's job. Kendall, thought to be behind Sunderland's Ken Knighton on the Rovers shortlist, said he was happy at Stoke in his player-coach role. He later changed his mind and decided to move to Rovers as the new player-manager in July.

SATURDAY 29TH MAY 1971

Hellas Verona came to Stoke in the initial group stages of the Anglo-Italian Cup and were beaten 2-0 thanks to goals from John Ritchie and Stewart Jump, a defender who played 61 games in four years.

TUESDAY 29TH MAY 1979

Alan Durban said he would like to talk to his former club Derby County about their vacant manager's job. In the end, the position at the Baseball Ground went to Colin Addison and Durban stayed in the Potteries for two more years before moving to Sunderland in 1981.

THURSDAY 30TH MAY 1968

Antipodean midfielder David Oldfield was born in Perth in Western Australia. He came to England to pursue a career as a professional footballer and Brian Little brought him to Stoke in 1998, at 30 years of age, having served Luton Town, Manchester City and Leicester City, respectively. After 74 games and seven goals, he moved on to Peterborough United in March 2000, then to Oxford United before retiring in 2004.

MONDAY 31st MAY 1948

Jackie Marsh, Stoke City's League Cup-winning full-back, was born in Newcastle-under-Lyme. Marsh, with 433 appearances, lies eighth in the all-time list (excluding wartime matches). The top ten are: Eric Skeels 606, John McCue 542, Bob McGrory 511, Denis Smith 493, Alan Bloor 484, Peter Fox 477, Tony Allen 473, Marsh, Frank Bowyer 436 and Frank Mountford 425.

WEDNESDAY 31st MAY 1967

The Cleveland Stokers played Cagliari, representing Chicago Mustangs, and drew 1-1 in the United Soccer Association. Mike Bernard gave Stoke the lead in the first half before British forward Gerry Hitchin equalised for the Italian side in the second half.

SATURDAY 1st JUNE 1968

Tom Jones' single 'Delilah' hit the number one spot in the US charts, after reaching number six in the UK. The song was adopted by Stoke fans in the 1980s after they were asked to tone down the singing in a pub, and it went on to become a club anthem.

TUESDAY 1st JUNE 1971

The bad feeling from the AS Roma match at the Victoria Ground paled into insignificance after events at the Olympic Stadium in Rome. Stoke had won the match 1-0 after a John Ritchie shot from Mike Pejic's cross. The crowd of 37,460 did not take the defeat well and started fighting with the soldiers on duty at the ground, throwing bottles and stones and letting off rockets and firecrackers! Due to the riot the Stoke players were not allowed out of the dressing room for two hours. They were eventually smuggled out of the ground.

THURSDAY 2nd JUNE 1921

Donald Clegg was born in Huddersfield and later started his career with the romantically-named Imperial Chemical Industries FC. After joining the Potters from Bury on a free transfer, he started the 1950/51 season as first choice goalkeeper ahead of Dennis Herod and Norman Wilkinson. After two defeats, to Newcastle United and Huddersfield Town, he was dropped by Bob McGrory and never played for Stoke again.

TUESDAY 2nd JUNE 1964

Mark Walters was born in Aston. The winger came on loan to Stoke during 1994 having served Aston Villa, Glasgow Rangers and Liverpool, and went on to score two goals in nine appearances.

MONDAY 3rd JUNE 1935

After more than 11 years as manager, Tom Mather left the club to take the hot seat at Newcastle United. Mather had taken over from Jock Rutherford in 1923 and left an established top-flight side boasting quality players. He was succeeded by full-back Bob McGrory.

FRIDAY 3RD JUNE 1960

At just 35-years-old, Tony Waddington became one of the youngest managers in the league when he took over from Frank Taylor whose contract had not been renewed at the end of the season. Waddington had joined the club in 1952 as a coach of the young players and had progressed to be assistant manager to Taylor by 1957. The trainer Norman Tapken also left the club as part of the management reshuffle.

SUNDAY 4TH JUNE 1967

Boston Rovers, more commonly known as Shamrock Rovers, played the Stokers in the United Soccer Association. Maurice Setters scored the only goal of the game for Cleveland as they maintained their unbeaten record in the tournament.

FRIDAY 4TH JUNE 1971

The Anglo-Italian Cup produced another hot tempered game as Stoke lost 2-1 at Hellas Verona and failed to qualify for the next stage of the competition. There were certainly very few 'Gentlemen of Verona' as referee Keith Walker appeared to be intimidated by the Verona players. John Ritchie scored for Stoke late on but Sergio Clerici had already scored two penalties, after what the City players considered to be acting on his behalf to win the spot kicks.

SATURDAY 4TH JUNE 1988

Arsenal signed Stoke centre-half Steve Bould, with the fee set by tribunal at £390,000, after City had offered him a long-term deal in an attempt to keep him at the club. Bould made 211 appearances for the Potters, and went on to win league medals, a FA Cup winners' medal, European medals and England caps whilst with the Gunners.

MONDAY 5TH JUNE 1972

Valerio Spadoni scored two goals on his debut for AS Roma as they avenged the 1-0 defeat from the previous year's Anglo-Italian Cup in the first group match. The 2-0 scoreline sent the Romans home happy and there were no repeats of the previous year's trouble.

WEDNESDAY 6TH JUNE 1979

Dean Crowe, Stoke's 5ft 5in striker, was born in Stockport. Crowe fell out of favour under Brian Little and Gudjon Thordarsson and moved on to Luton Town in 2001 after loan spells at Bury and Northampton Town. 'Deano' played 67 games for Stoke City, mostly as a substitute, scoring 13 goals in the process.

TUESDAY 7TH JUNE 1949

Luigi 'Lou' Macari was born in Edinburgh, before moving west to Glasgow to turn professional with Celtic. After a sparkling playing career with Celtic and Manchester United, totalling 154 goals in 506 games, Macari turned his hand to management at Swindon Town, West Ham United, Birmingham City and then Stoke City. He brought silverware and promotion to Stoke after joining in 1991, and then returned in 1994 after a spell as Celtic boss. Always in the headlines, Macari was involved in a betting scandal whilst at Swindon Town and also ended up in court with his former employers Celtic. In his two spells as manager Macari won 102 of his 237 games in charge, losing just 67.

SUNDAY 7TH JUNE 1970

"The greatest save ever made" was how Pelé described the one made by Gordon Banks in the World Cup group game in Guadalajara, Mexico. Banks, the only player to play for England in the World Cup Finals whilst at Stoke City, had only a split second to dive right, down and backwards to keep out the ball and halt the legendary Brazilian's celebrations, which were already in full flow.

TUESDAY 7TH JUNE 1988

Young Stoke midfielder Carl Beeston won his first England under-21 cap against Russia in the Toulon Tournament in France.

THURSDAY 7TH JUNE 2007

Chairman Peter Coates announced that the club had reached a deal to buy the Britannia Stadium. Stoke were set to invest £6m to purchase those shares of the ground which were owned by the City Council and by Stoke-on-Trent Regeneration.

WEDNESDAY 8TH JUNE 1910

In County Durham, future Stoke goalkeeper Norman Wilkinson was born. Initially a centre-half, he went in goal as an emergency and stayed there. Signing for the Potters in July 1935 for £100 from Huddersfield Town, Wilkinson stayed for a total of 17 years as first choice until the war, but as cover for Denis Herod afterwards. He played in 212 first-team matches keeping 49 clean sheets.

THURSDAY 8TH JUNE 1972

Stoke made a six-figure bid for Huddersfield Town striker Frank Worthington. They appeared to lose out to Liverpool but Frank's love of the high-life caused them to pull out and he moved to Leicester City.

WEDNESDAY 9TH JUNE 1926

Former Potters forward Bob Whittingham – who also played for Port Vale and Chelsea – collapsed and died at home from respiratory illness aged 37. During the war he scored 86 goals in 84 matches for Stoke, but did not recapture that form in peacetime.

WEDNESDAY 9TH JUNE 1965

Former Stoke outside-left Harold Hardman died in Sale aged 83. Hardman made 55 appearances for the Potters between 1910 and 1913, scoring 10 goals. In 1908 he was part of the Olympic gold medal-winning Great Britain football team which had defeated Denmark 2-0 in the final at White City. Whilst still playing at Stoke, he had become a director at Manchester United and went on to become chairman from 1951 to 1965, although he did not travel to Belgrade in February 1958 and avoided the Munich air disaster.

SATURDAY 10TH JUNE 1967

In 90-degree heat in Cleveland, Stoke played ADO Den Haag from Holland in the United Soccer Association. The Dutch, playing as San Francisco Golden Gate Gales, were no match for the Cleveland Stokers who won 4-1 thanks to a Peter Dobing brace and one each for Maurice Setters and Roy Vernon. The result left Stoke top of the Eastern Division with eight points.

SATURDAY 10TH JUNE 1972

The Anglo-Italian Cup once more produced a hot tempered match between Stoke and AS Roma at the Victoria Ground. Stoke lost the match 2-1 with John Ritchie scoring, but the real drama centred around the three early red cards. Both Peter Dobing and Denis Smith received their marching orders for Stoke and Morini of Roma also had an early bath.

TUESDAY 11TH JUNE 1963

John Dreyer, who played for Stoke after six years at Luton Town, was born in Alnwick in Northumberland. The centre-half was displaced in the Potters side by Larus Sigurdsson before moving on to Bradford City having made 60 appearances, scoring four goals.

MONDAY 12TH JUNE 1939

One of the most colourful characters in Stoke's history, Billy Rowley, died in the United States aged 73. He left after only one season with Stoke to play for Port Vale in 1884, but tried to return in 1886 only to have Vale block the transfer in the courts, along with that of George Bateman, but they both still moved across the Potteries. Rated as an excellent goalkeeper, he won two England caps, and appeared 143 times for the Potters including the first Football League fixture in 1888. Rowley took over as Stoke manager in 1895 but in 1898 he transferred himself to Leicester Fosse, giving himself a signing-on fee despite having returned to amateur status a few years previously. This transfer was also cancelled and he was suspended by the FA for 12 months.

THURSDAY 12TH JUNE 1947

In an incredible piece of timing, Frank Mountford handed in a transfer request just two days before the biggest match in Stoke's history, the title decider at Bramall Lane. He left the club in 1978.

SATURDAY 13TH JUNE 1908

Wolverhampton was the birthplace of Arthur Lewis who played in 170 games in goal for Stoke from 1929-1936, keeping 44 clean sheets.

MONDAY 13TH JUNE 1988

Home-grown winger Phil Heath moved to Oxford United in a deal worth £80,000. During Longton-born Heath's eight years on the books at Stoke he amassed 179 appearances, scoring 19 goals.

SATURDAY 14TH JUNE 1947

Stoke travelled to Bramall Lane knowing that a victory would see them crowned as the Football League champions on goal average above Liverpool. The heavy pitch conditions did not help and City had to come from behind through Alec Ormston to be level 1-1 at half-time. John McCue slipped soon after the break and Jack Pickering put Sheffield 2-1 up. Roared on by a travelling support of 10,000 in the 30,000 strong crowd, Stoke dominated the rest of the game but could find no way through, despite George Mountford hitting the bar and Freddie Steele's header stopping in the mud on the line. Liverpool claimed the championship and Stoke finished fourth, their joint-highest league position.

WEDNESDAY 14TH JUNE 1967

Aberdeen, playing as the Washington Whips in the United Soccer Association, came from 2-0 down with only 17 minutes to earn a draw against Cleveland Stokers. Stoke, who were ahead through Peter Dobing and George Eastham, tired rapidly in the intense heat.

TUESDAY 14TH JUNE 1988

The *Evening Sentinel* reported that Stoke manager Mick Mills was in talks with Manchester City forward Imre Varadi with a view to bringing the striker to Stoke. The 29-year-old Varadi, who also spoke to John Rudge at Port Vale, joined Sheffield Wednesday instead.

WEDNESDAY 14TH JUNE 2006

After an absence of only one year, Tony Pulis returned to the club as manager. The new chairman Peter Coates had a good working relationship with Pulis, and he was always the firm favourite to get the job. Coates said he would back Pulis with money to build the team and Pulis asked for patience from the fans while he did it.

TUESDAY 15TH JUNE 1965

Peter Dobing and Calvin Palmer both rejected the new contracts they were offered and were placed on the transfer list by the club, although both players eventually signed new contracts.

WEDNESDAY 16TH JUNE 1908

Due to the state of the club's finances and the failure of efforts to rally support, Mr Cowlishaw, the Stoke chairman, resigned the club's membership of the league and placed the company into liquidation. This move sparked strong local feeling and a group of local men raised the cash to resurrect the club. Led by Alfred Barker, a league referee from Shelton, the new Stoke Football Club (1908) Ltd came into existence.

MONDAY 16TH JUNE 1969

In Barnsley, South Yorkshire, Mark Crossley was born. The Welsh international joined City on loan from Middlesbrough in 2002/03 and his outstanding displays were key in maintaining Stoke's First Division status. He played in only 12 games but kept 7 clean sheets.

SATURDAY 17TH JUNE 1967

The Cleveland Stokers welcomed Dallas Tornado, also known as Dundee United, for the United Soccer Association game. Stoke ran out 4-1 winners thanks to two from Harry Burrows, and one each from Peter Dobing and Eric Skeels. The 10,132 crowd were lost in the 78,000 capacity stadium, and Stoke were now firm favourites for a place in the final with only five matches to play.

WEDNESDAY 18TH JUNE 2008

With Ricardo Fuller injured, Demar Phillips was the only Stoke player on show as Jamaica beat the Bahamas 6-0 in a World Cup qualifier. Also appearing for the Reggae Boyz was Rudolph Austin. He was denied a work permit to join Stoke in 2007, but a year later a fee of around £1m was agreed with Portmore United and a work permit was again applied for. Stoke had fallen foul of work permit regulations before: in 1982 the Swede Robert Prytz joined Glasgow Rangers after being denied a work permit.

WEDNESDAY 19TH JUNE 1946

Future darling of the Boothen End, Jimmy Greenhoff, was born in Barnsley. Jimmy joined the Potters for £100,000 – after playing for Leeds United and Birmingham City – which broke the club's transfer record and was the first time Stoke had paid out a six-figure fee for a player. Greenhoff scored 97 goals in his City career of 338 matches, before being sold to Manchester United in 1977, against his wishes, in order to bring in money to repair the Butler Street Stand. At United he won an FA Cup winners' medal in 1979 and also played alongside his brother, Brian.

TUESDAY 19TH JUNE 1962

Paul Bracewell was born in Heswall on the Wirral before coming through the ranks at Stoke. 'Brace' appeared in nearly 150 games for Stoke before following Alan Durban to Sunderland in 1983. He went on to win three full England caps, appeared in the successful Everton title winning side of the mid-eighties and was runner-up in no less than four FA Cup finals – three with Everton, one with Sunderland.

MONDAY 19TH JUNE 2006

Ex-Juventus and St Etienne striker Vincent Pericard signed a three-year contract on a free transfer from Portsmouth. The Cameroonian followed new boss Tony Pulis to the Britannia after just finishing a loan spell with him at Plymouth Argyle.

TUESDAY 20TH JUNE 1871

Centre-forward Thomas Hill, who scored two goals in only five games, was born in Market Drayton. After signing from his home-town club, he never settled in the Potteries and quickly moved on to play for Leicester Nomads before retiring 18 months later.

FRIDAY 20TH JUNE 1975

Kofi Nyamah was born in Islington, London. The midfielder never really made an impact at Stoke, or at his next club Luton Town, and quickly dropped back into non-league football from where Lou Macari had plucked him just two years earlier at Kettering Town.

THURSDAY 21st JUNE 1951

'The Working Man's Ballet' was the name of Alan Hudson's autobiography and that was exactly how he played the game. Born on this day in Chelsea, Hudson was a masterful midfielder who somehow only won two England caps, although his enjoyment of the high-life may have had an impact on that. During his two spells in the Potteries, 'Huddy' played 162 games, scored 9 goals and created many others. Stoke signed him twice from the same club, Chelsea.

THURSDAY 21st JUNE 1973

Peter Thorne was born in Manchester. Chic Bates paid £500,000 to Swindon Town to acquire the services of Thorne in the summer of 1997, and he went on to score 79 goals, including four hat-tricks, in 188 appearances before moving to Cardiff City for £1.7m in 2001.

WEDNESDAY 22nd JUNE 1988

Stoke signed Sheffield United winger Peter Beagrie for £215,000 from under the noses of Aston Villa and Derby County. Beagrie quickly became a fans' favourite with his jinking runs and somersault goal celebrations. He could also be frustrating by trying to beat his man too many times before crossing, and this was the reason Mick Mills gave for selling him to Everton for £750,000 just over a year later, after 61 games and eight goals.

SUNDAY 23rd JUNE 1872

Fred Gee was born in Handsworth in Birmingham. Gee made his debut in the last match of the first Football League season when Stoke were consigned to the wooden spoon, and went on to make 21 appearances.

THURSDAY 23rd JUNE 2005

Tony Pulis started to build his side for the 2005/06 season by signing Mamady Sidibe from Gillingham, not knowing he was actually building a side for Johan Boskamp. The 6ft 2in Malian international striker was not a prolific scorer at Gillingham, scoring only 13 times in 115 games, but Stoke fans soon saw his contribution to the side.

MONDAY 24TH JUNE 1985

Former England full-back Mick Mills joined Stoke City on a two year deal as player-manager. The former Ipswich and Southampton player, who won 42 England caps, took his first managerial job with the Potters.

TUESDAY 25TH JUNE 1946

The much-travelled forward John Tudor was born in Ilkeston. Widely known for playing well over 200 matches and scoring 73 times for Newcastle United, many alongside Malcolm MacDonald, Tudor joined Stoke from the St James' Park for £30,000 in 1976. He went on to play in 31 games, scoring 3 goals, before moving to Belgium.

SUNDAY 25TH JUNE 1967

In the United Soccer Association tournament in the USA, Stoke suffered their first defeat at the hands of Cerro from Uruguay. The South Americans, playing as New York Skyliners, won 2-1 as goals from Benedicto Ribiero and Juan Pintos cancelled out Peter Dobing's strike. The match ended with the Stoke side up in arms due to the Uruguayan tactics of diving and also down to ten men as John Mahoney had been sent off.

TUESDAY 26TH JUNE 2007

The club ended their time with Puma and signed a record-breaking new deal with kit producers Le Coq Sportif, for replica and team kits.

TUESDAY 27TH JUNE 1967

The Houston Stars, who were the Bangu Atletico Clube from Rio, inflicted the Cleveland Stokers' second defeat, and the second in two days, in the United Soccer League tournament. The match in Houston ended up 2-1 with Peter Dobing scoring Stoke's only goal.

TUESDAY 27TH JUNE 2006

Frank Mountford, ex-player and coach, died aged 83. A utility player who filled many positions, Mountford played over 600 games for the Potters including wartime matches, and despite not being born locally he was a part of the '£10 team'. Mountford, who scored a record 20 penalties for Stoke, went on to be a club coach until the late 1970s.

TUESDAY 28TH JUNE 1988

Mick Mills signed combative midfielder Chris Kamara from Swindon Town. Kamara was a controversial figure having being involved in a fracas that resulted in Leicester's Jim Melrose having a fractured cheekbone. The much-travelled player, who scored 7 goals in 71 games, later became manager of the Potters.

TUESDAY 28TH JUNE 2005

Despite having just signed a new deal to stay as manager, Tony Pulis was sacked by the Icelandic board, and left with a record of 44 wins in 122 league matches. There were tensions between board and manager regarding transfer policy and using the foreign markets. Johan Boskamp was installed as manager with the promise of exciting football and won 17 of his 46 league games in charge.

THURSDAY 29TH JUNE 2006

Sambegou Bangoura, the club's then-record signing, failed to turn up for pre-season training. It was not the first time: he turned up late when he first signed for the club and then went AWOL after the African Nations Cup in January.

THURSDAY 30TH JUNE 1966

At Trent Bridge in the third test against the West Indies, Arthur Jepson walked out to stand as a test match umpire for the first time. Jepson had a number of sporting careers as a first-class cricketer with Nottinghamshire, a test and one-day international umpire, and as a goalkeeper. Jepson signed for the Potters from Port Vale for £3,750 in June 1946 and made 32 appearances, keeping seven clean sheets, before moving to Lincoln City in December 1948.

FRIDAY 30TH JUNE 1967

Carl Beeston, a talented but injury-prone midfielder, was born in Stoke-on-Trent. Despite missing the entire 1986/87 season with glandular fever, Beeston made a total of 271 appearances for his home-town club. Capped at England under-21 level, Beeston missed out on the Autoglass Trophy Final at Wembley after picking up red cards in two successive matches.

SATURDAY 1st JULY 1967

Toronto City, aka Hibernian, were beaten 2-0 in the United Soccer Association. A crowd of 7,871 saw Peter Dobing and Harry Burrows give Stoke the victory and all but seal a place in the final. Only a disaster would now prevent Cleveland Stokers meeting Los Angeles Wolves – Wolverhampton Wanderers – in the final.

THURSDAY 1st JULY 1976

The Stoke squad arrived back from a tour of the Far East where Spurs and Northern Ireland goalkeeper Pat Jennings played two games as a guest player. The Stoke City friendly fixture list was certainly congested throughout the 1960s and 1970s. Tours were undertaken to places like South America, Australasia, USA, the Far East, Spain, Turkey and Africa, whilst the Victoria Ground hosted teams of the calibre of Benfica, Real Madrid, Santos, and Moscow Dynamo.

THURSDAY 2nd JULY 1964

Centre-half Ian Cranson was born in Easington, County Durham. The fans' favourite was signed from Sheffield Wednesday, for a then club-record £450,000 by Mick Mills, who knew him from their time together at Ipswich. Cranson suffered many injury problems but despite this he formed a great defensive partnership with Vince Overson. Having scored 12 goals in 281 games for Stoke he was forced to retire for good in 1996. He also went in goal for over an hour in the 2-1 win at Oldham Athletic after an injury to Mark Prudhoe.

WEDNESDAY 2nd JULY 1997

George Antonio, originally George Rowlands, died in Oswestry aged 82. Antonio joined Stoke from Oswestry Town for £200 in 1936 as an inside-forward and was one of few players to represent Stoke before, during and after the war. He left for Derby County in 1947 for £5,000.

WEDNESDAY 2nd JULY 2008

Prime Minister Gordon Brown praised Stoke City for reaching the Premiership during Prime Minister's Question Time in the House of Commons, after a question concerning the Gordon Banks statue.

THURSDAY 3RD JULY 1952

Former Stoke City and West Bromwich Albion half-back George Baddeley died aged 78. Baddeley played for Stoke from 1901 to 1908, along with his brother Amos, and other family members Sam and Tom. He made 225 appearances for the club, scoring 19 goals, before joining the Baggies for £250 when Stoke went to the wall in 1908.

WEDNESDAY 4TH JULY 1973

In Akureyri, Iceland, Larus Orri Sigurdsson was born. Sigurdsson came over to Stoke to keep himself fit for Iceland's under-21 internationals at the request of his cousin, Stoke midfielder Toddy Orlygsson. Lou Macari liked what he saw and signed Sigurdsson for £150,000 from Thor FC. The Icelandic centre-half made 228 Stoke appearances, scoring seven goals, before joining West Bromwich Albion for £325,000. 'Siggy' also played 42 times for his country.

WEDNESDAY 4TH JULY 2007

Academy product Martin Paterson rejected a contract offer and signed for newly-promoted Scunthorpe United. He then joined Burnley.

FRIDAY 5TH JULY 1957

Peter Fox, long-serving Stoke goalkeeper, was born in Scunthorpe. 'Foxy' made his debut for Sheffield Wednesday aged just 15 years and eight months, before moving to Stoke in 1978. He soon displaced Roger Jones from the side and went on to be a loyal servant to the Potters despite several back injuries and nearly quitting after being sent off against Luton Town. Once on the verge of an England call, Fox holds Stoke's goalkeeping appearance record at 477 games, and kept the record number of clean sheets with 139 in his 15 years of service.

WEDNESDAY 5TH JULY 1967

A 0-0 draw with Glentoran – Detroit Cougars – pushed Stoke a little closer to the United Soccer Association Championship match against the winner of the Western Division. The match was fairly uneventful – except for the sending off of Bill Bentley and Glentoran's Danny Trainor – and kept Stoke on top of the Eastern Division.

TUESDAY 6TH JULY 1976

To Irish parents, Rory Delap was born in Sutton Coldfield. Delap came from Sunderland, on loan at first, but broke his leg in only his second game, ironically against Sunderland. He made a full comeback and went on to play a vital role in the promotion year of 2007/08 with his long throws which caused havoc in opposition defences. He ended the season as captain.

THURSDAY 6TH JULY 2006

Defender Andy Wilkinson, from Stone, signed a new two-year deal with Stoke. Despite a number of injuries in his early career, 'Wilko' became an important squad player after going out for loan spells at Telford United, Partick Thistle, Shrewsbury Town and Blackpool.

WEDNESDAY 7TH JULY 1954

Welsh midfielder Mickey Thomas was born in Mochdre, Powys. Stoke signed the ex-Manchester United star from Brighton & Hove Albion in August 1982 for £200,000 and he quickly became popular with the fans. He became a victim of Richie Barker's change of tactics and moved to Chelsea in January 1984 for a fee of £75,000. Thomas returned to the Potteries in the early 1990s before heading back to Wrexham, where he started his career. Jailed for handling fake money in 1993, Thomas played 120 games for Stoke, scoring 22 goals for the club.

MONDAY 7TH JULY 2008

Former Stoke City midfielder Neil Mackenzie finally lost on the Channel 4 quiz show *Countdown* after five winning days. His appearance made headlines as he was the first professional footballer to appear on the show. The much-travelled Birmingham-born player had played 46 times for Stoke scoring a single goal, before moving to Cambridge.

SATURDAY 8TH JULY 2006

Coach Mark O'Connor, former Gillingham and Bournemouth winger, left Plymouth Argyle and followed Tony Pulis to the Britannia Stadium. The management team was completed by former Argyle, Oxford United and Norkopping manager Dave Kemp, as Pulis' assistant.

TUESDAY 8th JULY 2008

The Austin Aztex secured a spot in the Mid-South Divisional play-offs after beating Mississippi Brilla 1-0. The Aztex franchise was purchased by Stoke's US-based director Phil Rawlins, and he immediately started to forge strong links between the two clubs. Former Potters forward Adrian Heath was appointed as manager of the Aztex and Stoke should benefit from summer training camps and player exchanges in both directions.

SUNDAY 9th JULY 1967

A 3-1 defeat in the United Soccer Association to Sunderland, playing as Vancouver Royal Canadians, left Stoke top of the Eastern Division by virtue of goal average. This should have been enough to qualify for the championship match. However, Aberdeen lodged an appeal regarding Wolves' use of substitutes early on in the tournament and the match needed to be replayed the next night. An Aberdeen victory would knock Stoke out, after they had looked promising.

WEDNESDAY 9th JULY 1980

Derby County paid £25,000 to take goalkeeper Roger Jones to the Baseball Ground. Jones had played 112 games since signing from Newcastle United on a free transfer in 1977 and kept a club record of 20 clean sheets in the league in the 1978/79 promotion season.

MONDAY 10th JULY 1967

Aberdeen beat Wolves 3-0 in the replayed United Soccer Association match, which had originally finished 1-1, and qualified for the championship match at the expense of Stoke. The Cleveland Stokers had played some good football but they had not done quite enough.

THURSDAY 11th JULY 1985

Stoke's plans to build an ASDA supermarket on the ground behind the Boothen End were rejected by the City Council. Chairman Sandy Clubb had pushed for the plan as it was a way to secure the financial future of the club, but the project would get no further than this point. This loss of funds was another body blow for the recently relegated club.

SATURDAY 12TH JULY 1941

John Ritchie was born in Kettering. 'Big John' signed for Stoke from his home-town club in 1961 for just £2,500. Over the next 13 years he gave tremendous service to the Potters, except for a three-year spell at Sheffield Wednesday in the late 1960s. Ritchie scored 176 goals for Stoke and finished just five short of Freddie Steele's all-time league goals record on 135. After running a successful pottery business, Ritchie died in February 2007, and was immortalised with a bust behind the new Boothen End at the Britannia Stadium.

FRIDAY 12TH JULY 1985

Mick Mills appointed former Wolves manager Cyril 'Sammy' Chung as his new coach. Chung stayed at Stoke until the autumn of 1989.

SATURDAY 12TH JULY 2008

Archbishop Desmond Tutu and Pelé visited the Britannia Stadium to unveil a monument entitled 'A Hero Who Could Fly' in honour of Gordon Banks. A charity football match then followed with a Gordon Banks XI playing a Pelé XI, both made up of footballers and actors.

FRIDAY 13TH JULY 1883

On this most superstitious of days, William Harding – brought to the club from Wolstanton – played for Stoke during their Birmingham & District League campaign of 1908/09. After just five appearances at right-half, he was ousted by Sam Baddeley and moved to Ribbendale.

MONDAY 14TH JULY 2008

As the countdown continued to Stoke City's debut Premiership season there were a great many transfer rumours circulating between the fans and the Potters were linked to just about every player on the market. One rumour which had some plausibility, was linking the club with Liverpool and England goalkeeper Scott Carson. Tony Pulis confirmed that the club had an offer accepted for the 22-year-old, which was believed to be over £3m. Other names linked included Thomas Gravesen, Anthony Gardner, Marton Fulop, Lee McCulloch, David Nugent, Dean Whitehead and Jon Walters.

MONDAY 15TH JULY 1929

Bobby Howitt, a half-back who was never very popular at Stoke, was born in Glasgow. Despite his lack of popularity, he was hard working and won a Second Division championship medal with the Potters in 1962/63. He played in 150 games for Stoke, scoring 16 goals, and then managed Motherwell. He sadly died in 2005 from Alzheimer's disease.

TUESDAY 15TH JULY 1930

Brian Doyle was born in Manchester. He made just 19 appearances at full-back in the early 1950s before moving on to Exeter City. After hanging up his boots he became a manager, first at Workington and then Stockport County, where he led the Cheshire club to bottom place in the Football League in 1974.

TUESDAY 16TH JULY 1957

Etruria was the location for the birth of Albert Sturgess. The full-back moved to Sheffield United when Stoke went out of business in 1908 and went on to win an FA Cup winners medal and two England caps. For the Potters, he scored 4 goals in 135 appearances.

FRIDAY 16TH JULY 1976

Product of the youth system Sean Haslegrave moved to Nottingham Forest in a deal worth £35,000. During his eight-year career with Stoke, he found his first team opportunities limited and mainly acted as cover for the first choice players. Despite this, he played in 142 games for Stoke.

MONDAY 16TH JULY 1979

The newly promoted Stoke squad reported back for pre-season training with manager Alan Durban. Amongst them was new signing Loek Ursem who had signed during the summer for £85,000 from AZ '67 Alkmaar. Ursem was Stoke's first foreign import and went on to make 44 appearances, scoring seven goals. He should have been preceded in 1965 by Swede Sven Larsson who played for Stoke in a friendly against Moscow Dynamo. As he was unregistered, City were fined £105 and eventually permission to sign him was refused.

SUNDAY 17TH JULY 1938

John Hall was born in Hucknall. The centre-forward – who had trials at both Mansfield Town and Nottingham Forest before signing for Stoke in 1904 – scored 18 times in 55 outings for the Potters. After leaving the Potters he played for Brighton & Hove Albion, Middlesbrough, Leicester Fosse and Birmingham City. After hanging up his boots he went on to successfully coach Feyenoord in Holland.

FRIDAY 18TH JULY 1952

Half-back George Baddeley died in West Bromwich, where he had become a publican after retiring from football in May 1914.

FRIDAY 18TH JULY 2003

John Eustace joined Stoke from Coventry City on a free transfer and looked like a very good acquisition. Unfortunately, serious knee trouble restricted his career at the Britannia Stadium. Ironically, he was just starting to find his pre-injury form again when he was sold to promotion rivals Watford in January 2008 having played 84 times for the Potters, scoring six goals.

FRIDAY 18TH JULY 2008

Stoke City smashed their record transfer fee by paying £5.5m for the services of striker Dave Kitson from Reading, who had just been relegated to the Championship. Kitson was a proven goalscorer at Premiership level and had been close to making Fabio Capello's England squad. The signing was the first as City prepared for life in the Premiership and signalled their intent to stay up. The previous record fee was the £1.2m paid for Leon Cort in the previous January.

MONDAY 19TH JULY 1915

After an absence of seven seasons, Stoke were elected back into the Football League at the expense of Glossop North End. World War I meant the club had to wait a further four years until 1919 to regain their league status. Along with Stoke, the other newcomers in the expanded post war league were Coventry City, Rotherham County, South Shields – later Gateshead – and West Ham United.

TUESDAY 19TH JULY 2005

Manchester United signed 22-year-old goalkeeper Ben Foster for an initial fee of £1m, although with additional clauses surrounding appearances and England caps there was the potential to bring the total up to £3m. The deal was even more remarkable as Foster, who had signed three years earlier from Racing Club Warwick, had yet to make a first team appearance for Stoke, despite plenty of time on the bench. United immediately sent Foster out to Watford on loan.

FRIDAY 20TH JULY 2007

The final pre-season friendly before heading off to the now-regular summer training camp in Austria was against Macclesfield Town at their Moss Rose ground. Honours were even as the match ended 1-1 but the Potters must have been worried that midfielder Rory Delap had to be substituted for exhaustion after only 28 minutes. The match against the Silkmen followed the annual visit to Newcastle Town.

WEDNESDAY 21ST JULY 1926

Full-back Cyril Watkin was born in Stoke. Watkin's career was ended by a broken leg soon after Stoke sold him to Bristol City for £8,000 in July 1952. He made a total of 90 outings for Stoke without scoring a single goal. City recruited him after a brief spell at Port Vale.

TUESDAY 21ST JULY 1953

Brian Talbot, capped six times by England, was born in Ipswich. He joined the Potters for £25,000 from Watford in 1986, and made 64 appearances scoring seven goals. He then moved to West Bromwich Albion for £15,000 in 1988, where he became manager.

TUESDAY 22ND JULY 1980

Stoke chairman Tom Degg died in office aged 72. He had taken over from Albert Henshall, who was the club's most successful and second longest-serving chairman after Alderman Booth. Following Degg, there was a run of short-lived chairmen in Percy Axon, Frank Edwards and Sandy Clubb, before Peter Coates took control for the first time in 1986.

WEDNESDAY 23RD JULY 1941

Welsh international Joey Jones was born at Rhosymedre, near Wrexham. Known as 'The Old Warhorse', he lost the sight in one eye after heading a football. Jones made 129 appearances for the club, and played in a further 133 games during the war. Jones was signed from Treharris along with George Smart in 1911 and remained at the club until 1920, when he was sold to Crystal Palace for £150.

SATURDAY 23RD JULY 1955

Brendan O'Callaghan was born in Bradford, before starting his football career at Doncaster Rovers. 'Big Bren' moved to Oldham Athletic in 1985, but sustained a groin injury in his first game which he never really recovered from. After retirement he returned to the Victoria Ground to work as the Community Development Officer for the club.

WEDNESDAY 24TH JULY 1968

Danish international Henrik Risom was born. Risom signed for Stoke, aged 32, from Vejle Boldklub in his native Denmark in 2000. The midfielder was capped nine times by his country and was released by Stoke after just one season, making 34 appearances.

FRIDAY 25TH JULY 1980

Tottenham Hotspur clinched the signing of young starlet Garth Crooks from Stoke. The 22-year-old local lad, who had a difficult relationship with manager Alan Durban, moved to Spurs for £600,000 having scored 53 goals in 164 appearances for Stoke. At White Hart Lane, he formed a strong partnership with Steve Archibald and won two successive FA Cup winners medals in the early 1980s.

THURSDAY 25TH JULY 1985

Want-away winger Mark Chamberlain signed a weekly contract whilst waiting to see which club would make him an offer to return to top-flight football. Mick Mills was trying to persuade the England winger to stay at Stoke but he wanted to play in the First Division to increase his chances of making the 1986 World Cup squad. He signed for Sheffield Wednesday not long afterwards.

MONDAY 26TH JULY 1954

George Bridgett passed away aged 71. As a religious person, he would refuse to play on a holy day, and played only seven games for Stoke.

TUESDAY 27TH JULY 1976

Stoke suffered a major injury blow for the new season as Jimmy Robertson broke his leg whilst playing for Seattle in the States.

FRIDAY 27TH JULY 2007

Whilst on their pre-season training camp in Austria, Stoke played a friendly against the Galacticos of Real Madrid. Bernd Schuster's La Liga champions were given a good workout but they ran out 2-0 winners with goals from Raul and Soldado. The Madrid team also included other star names including Pepe, Cannavaro, Torres, Cicinho, Guti and Saviola. The injured Ruud van Nistelrooy claimed to have been most impressed by winger Peter Sweeney!

THURSDAY 28TH JULY 1966

New Stoke coach Alan Ball senior stated in the *Evening Sentinel* that his son would be a good acquisition for Stoke, just two days before he would take part in the World Cup Final at Wembley. Stoke had already had a bid of £100,000 rejected by Blackpool before the tournament started and would look to renew their interest after the final. Ball senior said he was telling Ball junior 'the truth' about the club, but that his presence may count against the Potters when it came to making the signing. Ball junior eventually joined Stoke as assistant to Mick Mills some 33 years later, before succeeding him as manager.

TUESDAY 29TH JULY 1980

Alan Durban had planned to use the money made from the sale of Garth Crooks to purchase Paul Maguire from Shrewsbury Town and Iain Munro from St Mirren. The deals seemed to have fallen apart as Maguire had gone to talk to Everton manager Gordon Lee and Iain Munro had injured himself in training in Scotland. Despite these hitches the deals would eventually go through.

SUNDAY 30TH JULY 1944

Sergeant with the Royal Warwickshire Regiment, Henry Salmon was killed in action in Caen, France. The former electrician turned professional with the Potters in 1932, before transferring to Millwall two years later. He made just three first-team appearances.

MONDAY 30TH JULY 2007

Midfielder Darel Russell returned to Norwich City for £410,000, four years after Stoke bought him from the Canaries for £125,000. The energetic midfielder made 182 appearances, scoring 16 goals while at the club.

SUNDAY 31ST JULY 1887

Tommy Broad was born in Stalybridge four years before his brother, Jimmy. Tommy was a good winger who could deliver inviting crosses, and Jimmy was a forward who could finish them. Jimmy scored 67 goals in 116 outings and Tommy scored 4 goals in 89 outings. Another brother, Wilf, played for Manchester City and Millwall.

WEDNESDAY 31ST JULY 1974

The only Stoke player to lift a trophy at the Millennium Stadium in Cardiff, Peter Handyside, was born in Dumfries. Handyside made most of his league appearances for Grimsby Town, but still managed to clock up 88 outings in his two years at Stoke.

FRIDAY 1st AUGUST 2003

Following the purchases of John Eustace, Clint Hill and Gifton Noel-Williams, Stoke made another splash in the transfer market signing Ed De Goey from Chelsea. The 36-year-old Dutch stopper, capped 31 times by his country, signed a two-year deal in order to get first team football. Chelsea had payed Feyenoord £2.25m for his services six years previously, but he had lost his place to Carlo Cudicini.

MONDAY 1st AUGUST 2005

Just prior to the start of the new season, club captain Clive Clarke joined West Ham United for £250,000 after 12 years and 264 games for the club. After leaving Stoke, Clive's career did not really take off and in August 2007 he collapsed at half-time whilst on loan at Leicester City. The heart failure he suffered ended his career. Clarke had played two full internationals for the Republic of Ireland.

MONDAY 2nd AUGUST 1954

Sammy McIlroy, the last Busby Babe, was born in Belfast. After playing for Manchester United for more than a decade, McIlroy moved to Stoke as their record purchase – costing £350,000 – as Bryan Robson arrived at United. McIlroy played 144 times for Stoke, scoring 14 goals, before moving on to Manchester City on a free transfer after Stoke were relegated from the First Division in 1985.

TUESDAY 2nd AUGUST 1966

The first link in Stoke's Icelandic connection, Thorvaldur 'Toddy' Orlygsson, was born in Odense in Denmark. Lou Macari snapped up Toddy from Nottingham Forest for £175,000 and he went on to make 110 appearances and score 19 goals for the club before moving to Oldham Athletic in 1995. He was capped a total of 41 times by Iceland before his retirement in 1999.

WEDNESDAY 3rd AUGUST 1960

Ernest Mullineux, who had been born in Northwood, died in Bucknall aged 81. Mullineux made 186 appearances for the club between 1906 and 1914 before transferring to Wellington Town.

WEDNESDAY 4TH AUGUST 1943

Keith Bebbington was born at Cuddington, near Nantwich, in Cheshire. Outside-left Bebbington was Stoke's first ever substitute in 1965. He scored 22 goals in 124 appearances for the Potters before moving on to Oldham Athletic in a joint deal with George Kinnell for a combined fee of £26,000 in 1966.

FRIDAY 5TH AUGUST 1972

The FA Cup third place play-off was essentially a pre-season match with little excitement for the near 24,000 present at St Andrew's, until the penalty shoot-out. Stoke lost the penalties 4-3 when Peter Dobing's kick was saved by Paul Cooper, and Birmingham City became the last team to finish third in the FA Cup.

SATURDAY 5TH AUGUST 2006

The first game of the season at Roots Hall ended in victory for Southend United. A solitary Freddy Eastwood goal ruined Tony Pulis' day in his first game in charge since returning as manager in the summer.

THURSDAY 6TH AUGUST 1936

England international defender George Shutt died in Hanley. Shutt received the distinction of being one of only two players – Elijah Smith being the other – who appeared in Stoke's first league match in 1888, as well as their first FA Cup match some five years earlier. He scored two goals in a total of 30 appearances for the Potters before he left to join Hanley Town in 1889. Later to play for Port Vale, he also became a Football League referee in 1891.

SATURDAY 6TH AUGUST 2005

Johan Boskamp's first game as a manager in English football, in front of 18,744 fans, ended 0-0, just like the previous season's 'binary football', but it was far from dull. Stoke were reduced to ten men after only 13 minutes as referee Mark Clattenburg sent off Gerry Taggart, yet should still have won the match as substitute Kevin Harper blasted a penalty over the bar with only 15 minutes left.

SATURDAY 7TH AUGUST 1999

For the opening day of the season at home to Oxford United, Stoke City wore squad numbers on their shirts for the first time, meaning the unusual sight of Kevin Keen running round in the number 30 shirt! Gary Megson's first game in charge of the Potters ended in a 2-1 defeat despite a Graham Kavanagh strike. There had been little transfer activity with only on-loan Sam Aiston to show for the summer movements.

MONDAY 8TH AUGUST 1983

Outside-left Joe Johnson died in West Bromwich where he had lived since retiring from football. Born in Grimsby, Johnson won five full England caps in the late 1930s and also played for Bristol City, West Bromwich Albion, Hereford United and Northwich Victoria.

SATURDAY 8TH AUGUST 1998

Northampton Town played host to Stoke on the first day of the new season as City got used to life in the third tier of English football. Brian Little's first game as the new Stoke boss saw goals from Graham Kavanagh, Peter Thorne and Dean Crowe help City to a comfortable 3-1 victory at the Sixfields Stadium. The match saw Potters debuts for Phil Robinson, Bryan Small and David Oldfield.

TUESDAY 8TH AUGUST 2007

Belgian international attacking full-back Carl Hoefkens joined West Bromwich Albion for a fee of £750,000 in a move which fans saw as Stoke selling their best players. Hoefkens had made 96 appearances after being signed by Johan Boskamp from Germinal Beerschot Belgium for £350,000 and scored five goals, two from the penalty spot.

TUESDAY 9TH AUGUST 1932

Johnny King was born near Nantwich, in Cheshire. King's career started at his local club Crewe Alexandra before he moved to Stoke. His forward partner at Gresty Road, Frank Blunstone, moved on to Chelsea and played for England. After leaving in 1961 for Cardiff City for a fee of £12,000, King returned to Crewe for five years before retiring in 1967.

SATURDAY 9TH AUGUST 1969

Having broken the club's transfer record to bring Jimmy Greenhoff from Birmingham City to Stoke, Tony Waddington threw him straight into the opening day match at Molineux. Greenhoff did not pay his £100,000 fee back immediately as he failed to score and Wolves eased to a 3-1 win, with Harry Burrows grabbing the Stoke goal. It would be in his fourth appearance nearly three weeks later that Greenhoff would break his duck, scoring at home to Coventry City.

SATURDAY 9TH AUGUST 1997

Having had to wait for his chance to manage Stoke while assistant manager to Lou Macari, Chic Bates then had to wait for his first home game in charge too as construction of the Britannia Stadium was being completed. Having special dispensation to play the first three league games away from home, Stoke travelled to St Andrew's to face Birmingham City on the opening day and lost to goals from Paul Devlin and Peter Ndlovu.

SATURDAY 10TH AUGUST 1968

The first game of the season saw Stoke host Sunderland. Peter Dobing and Willie Stevenson grabbed the goals as City took the points in front of 22,475. The 2-1 win would be one of only three in the first 12 matches as Stoke's season got off to a poor start.

SATURDAY 10TH AUGUST 2002

Newly-promoted Stoke City, with new boss Steve Cotterill at the helm, travelled to Hillsborough for the opening fixture. The Potters battled out a point from a goalless game against Sheffield Wednesday in front of 27,746 fans with the Owls having most of the play.

SATURDAY 11TH AUGUST 1973

Geoff Hurst scored the only goal as Stoke won their first Watney Cup match against Plymouth Argyle at Home Park. The competition was for the top scoring sides in each division who had not won promotion or qualified for European competition. Stoke progressed into the semi-final with this win.

SATURDAY 11TH AUGUST 2007

On-loan Manchester United defender Ryan Shawcross scored the only goal of the game, on his debut, as Stoke came away from Ninian Park with all three points on the opening day of the season. Cardiff City had a penalty saved by Steve Simonsen in the 88th minute. There were also debuts for new boy Richard Cresswell and on-loan Stephen Wright.

SUNDAY 12TH AUGUST 1962

Midfielder Nigel Gleghorn was born in Seaham, County Durham. The former Ipswich Town and Manchester City star followed manager Lou Macari and centre-half Vince Overson from Birmingham City for £100,000 in 1992. He went on to make 208 appearances for the Potters before being given a free transfer to Burnley in 1996 – again moving with Overson – and eventually retiring in 2004. Prior to Birmingham, 'Gleggy' had played for Ipswich and Manchester City.

TUESDAY 12TH AUGUST 1997

Stoke beat Rochdale 3-1 in the first leg of the Coca-Cola Cup first round tie at Spotland. Richard Forsyth scored Stoke's third from a corner, the first goal for the Potters from a corner since 1995/96.

FRIDAY 13TH AUGUST 1982

Stoke visited Vale Park for a friendly which they won 1-0. The match had other consequences, though, as Richie Barker was so impressed by certain members of the Vale squad that he soon went back to complete the signings of goalkeeper Mark Harrison, Mark Chamberlain and eventually Mark's brother, Neville Chamberlain.

WEDNESDAY 13TH AUGUST 2003

Sir Alex Ferguson and his Manchester United side visited Stoke for their final pre-season friendly, a rare one in England, and came off second best as Tony Pulis' side won 3-1. Marc Goodfellow grabbed a brace against eccentric French international keeper Fabien Barthez. Goodfellow's second goal was memorable as he chipped Barthez, who flung himself backwards to attempt a save, only for the ball to come back off the bar, hit Barthez on the head and fly in.

WEDNESDAY 14TH AUGUST 1968

West Ham United came to the Victoria Ground and took both points with a 2-0 victory. The result started a run of ten games in which the Potters would not score more than one goal in a game.

TUESDAY 14TH AUGUST 2007

Stoke bowed out of the Carling Cup on penalties in the first round at Spotland against a Rochdale side struggling at the foot of the Football League. City had lost in the first round of the competition in six of the last seven years, always to lower league opposition, and three times on penalties. On the same day, Sam Bangoura finally left the club for Boavista. His continued absences, due to passport problems and family issues, reducing his value to £270,000 from the €1.25m Stoke paid to Standard Liege for his services just two years before.

WEDNESDAY 15TH AUGUST 1973

The Watney Cup semi-final at the Victoria Ground saw Stoke triumph 4-1 against Bristol City. Geoff Hurst, Mike Pejic, Terry Conroy and Jimmy Greenhoff got the goals in front of 13,812.

SATURDAY 15TH AUGUST 1998

The first-ever league meeting between the two sides resulted in a 2-0 win for Stoke against Macclesfield Town at the Britannia Stadium, the goals scored by Dean Crowe and Peter Thorne in front of 13,981.

SATURDAY 16TH AUGUST 1969

In front of a crowd of over 23,000 at the Victoria Ground, John Ritchie and Peter Dobing scored to earn a 2-1 victory over West Ham United. This was Stoke's first win of the season after a defeat and a draw against Wolves and Nottingham Forest, respectively.

SATURDAY 16TH AUGUST 2003

Stoke defender Wayne Thomas won a dramatic game with a 90th minute header to put Stoke on top of the first published Division One table of the season. Wimbledon striker Patrick Agyemang had earlier scored to cancel out Carl Asaba's first-half penalty.

SATURDAY 17TH AUGUST 1974

The first day of the 1974/75 season saw the visit of Leeds United for Brian Clough's first game in charge of the Elland Road side. Cloughie did not get off to a good start as 33,534 cheered Stoke to a 3-0 victory thanks to John Mahoney, Jimmy Greenhoff and John Ritchie.

SATURDAY 17TH AUGUST 1985

After being relegated from the top division, Stoke opened the new campaign with a 3-1 home defeat to Sheffield United which extended their run of defeats to 11 matches – a club record. New manager Mick Mills needed to find a way to halt the slide, after Phil Heath scored Stoke's goal in front of a crowd of 11,679 at the Victoria Ground.

SATURDAY 17TH AUGUST 1991

After falling out with Birmingham City owners the Kumars, former Glasgow Celtic and Manchester United forward Lou Macari made his bow as Stoke manager at Valley Parade. It was not the perfect start as Stoke fell 1-0 to a Brian Tinnion goal for Bradford in the 17th minute.

SATURDAY 18TH AUGUST 1973

The Watney Cup Final was contested at the Victoria Ground and Stoke ran out 2-0 winners against Hull City thanks to a Jimmy Greenhoff brace. A crowd of over 18,000 turned out despite the match being televised, to see Stoke lift the trophy.

SATURDAY 18TH AUGUST 2007

Stoke hosted newly-relegated Charlton Athletic in their first home game of the season and ran out 2-1 winners. The result, thanks to goals for Ricardo Fuller and Jon Parkin, left Stoke on top of the Championship table as City started their promotion season as they meant to continue.

SATURDAY 19TH AUGUST 1939

The Football League Jubilee Fund game against Wolves saw Stoke players wearing numbers on their shirts for the first time after they were approved by the Football League. Tommy Sale, number nine, scored both Stoke goals in a 4-2 defeat at the Victoria Ground.

SATURDAY 19TH AUGUST 1967

Stoke started the season at Highbury and came away with nothing as Arsenal ran out 2-0 winners. Tony Waddington gave a baptism of fire to young full-back Jackie Marsh and did not even tell the tannoy announcer who was playing at right-back! Marsh only made two further starts in his debut season but would be a fixture in the team by the end of 1968/69. He went on to play for the club until 1978.

SATURDAY 19TH AUGUST 1989

After spending over £1m in the summer, the pressure was on Mick Mills and his men to deliver. On the opening day of the season Stoke hosted West Ham United and gave debuts to no fewer than four new signings; Wayne Biggins, Ian Cranson, Ian Scott and Derek Statham. The Potters rescued a point late on as Biggins scored on his debut, but they would not register their first win until 17th October.

SATURDAY 20TH AUGUST 1960

The Tony Waddington era started with the long journey to Plymouth Argyle for the first match of the season. 'Waddo' saw his new charges go down 3-1 with Peter Bullock claiming a consolation.

SATURDAY 20TH AUGUST 1966

Fresh from the World Cup-winning England squad – although not actually taking to the field – midfielder George Eastham made his Stoke debut after signing from Arsenal for a fee of £30,000. His debut came away to Nottingham Forest, a game that Stoke won 2-1 thanks to goals from Calvin Palmer and Peter Dobing at the City Ground.

SATURDAY 20TH AUGUST 1977

Stoke lost their first game in the Second Division after being defeated by 2-1 at Mansfield Town. The Stags' victory caused unrest and trouble amongst the Stoke supporters who were not happy.

SATURDAY 21ST AUGUST 1965

Keith Bebbington became the first-ever substitute used by the Potters when he replaced the injured Dennis Viollet at Highbury.

SATURDAY 21st AUGUST 1971

After two away games, Stoke's first home game of the campaign saw Crystal Palace visit the Potteries. The Eagles went home with nothing after a 3-1 defeat in which John Mahoney scored his first goal for three years, and Jimmy Greenhoff and John Ritchie grabbed the others.

TUESDAY 22nd AUGUST 1922

Long-serving John McCue was born in Longton. He went to Longton Council School before joining up with the Potters at 15-years-old. He left the club aged 38 and retired three years later.

TUESDAY 22nd AUGUST 2006

League Two Darlington came to the Britannia Stadium and knocked Stoke out of the Carling Cup at the first round stage, despite Stoke taking the lead through Vincent Pericard. Young full-back Carl Dickinson made his first cup appearance for the club in this match. 'Dicko' endeared himself to the City faithful with strong spirited, passionate football. It was Carl's celebration which adorned the national media after promotion to the Premiership in 2007/08.

SATURDAY 23rd AUGUST 1952

Sammy Smyth and Harry Oscroft got the new season off to a great start as the Potters beat Manchester City 2-1 in front of 35,006 at the Victoria Ground. The result was especially welcomed by Frank Taylor who had taken over from Bob McGrory after the Scotsman's 17 years in the hot seat. The once-capped England international full-back, who spent his playing career at Wolves before retiring aged just 28, would spend eight years in charge at Stoke before leaving.

SATURDAY 23rd AUGUST 1958

The first game of the season saw Stoke crumble 6-1 to Fulham at Craven Cottage in front of nearly 32,000 spectators. The Potters' goal was scored by Harry Oscroft, his 100th for the club, making him the sixth person to achieve that landmark. The results at the start of 1958/59 saw Stoke win their first four home games and lose their first three away.

SATURDAY 24TH AUGUST 1968

John Mahoney became the first substitute to score for the Potters, and it turned out to be the only goal of the game against Leicester City at the Victoria Ground. A crowd of 16,663 were there to see Tony Waddington's Stoke side register their second win of the new season.

SATURDAY 24TH AUGUST 1985

Mick Mills' Stoke finally avoided defeat at the 12th attempt by holding out for a 0-0 draw against Barnsley in front of 6,598 at Oakwell. The record of 11 consecutive losses still stands.

SATURDAY 25TH AUGUST 1923

After the short reign of John Rutherford, the Stoke directors turned to former Southend United manager Tom Mather to restore the club's status. Mather's 12 years in charge did not get off to a spectacular start as Leeds United came to the Victoria Ground and claimed a point after a 1-1 draw with an attendance of 20,000.

SATURDAY 25TH AUGUST 1928

Stoke got the new season off to a perfect start at the City Ground by beating their hosts 5-1. Nottingham Forest had no answer to Stoke's attacking football and were beaten by two goals from Charlie Wilson and one each for Harry Davies, Bobby Liddle and Walter Bussey.

MONDAY 26TH AUGUST 1963

Newly-promoted Stoke hit top spot in the First Division for the first time in 16 years. Peter Dobing grabbed two of Stoke's goals as they beat Aston Villa 3-1 at Villa Park in front of 39,041 spectators. Jackie Mudie made one of his final appearances for Stoke and netted the other goal.

SATURDAY 26TH AUGUST 1978

A Garth Crooks penalty sealed a 2-0 win against Millwall to put the Potters on top of the Second Division. Alan Durban's side would only fall out of the top three promotion places once again in the remainder of the 1978/79 season after this victory in front of 15,176 at the Victoria Ground.

MONDAY 26TH AUGUST 1985

Following five months and 12 matches without a victory, Stoke broke their duck in style by beating Leeds United 6-2 at the Victoria Ground in front of 7,047 fans. The result eased fears that City would go straight down, even though it would be eight games before their next victory. The win came courtesy of two goals each for Keith Bertschin and Mark Chamberlain and one each for Chris Maskery and George Berry.

MONDAY 27TH AUGUST 1934

A four-goal salvo from Stanley Matthews condemned Leeds United to an 8-1 defeat in the first home game of the season. A crowd of 24,555 saw Matthews and Joe Johnson rip through Leeds, with Johnson and Tommy Sale both scoring two each. Matthews was on his way to an England call.

WEDNESDAY 27TH AUGUST 1997

The first game at the new Britannia Stadium was the second leg of the Coca-Cola Cup first round tie against Rochdale. Leading 3-1 from the first leg, City could only draw 1-1 with Graham Kavanagh first to score at the new ground.

SUNDAY 28TH AUGUST 1971

Stoke took both points from Highbury as John Ritchie's 20th-minute shot gave City a 1-0 win against Arsenal. A gate of 37,637 was present to witness a masterclass in defending from Denis Smith and Alan Bloor. 'Bluto' Bloor played over 470 games for Stoke in 18 years on the books, mostly in partnership with Smith.

SATURDAY 28TH AUGUST 1982

The new season saw Stoke welcoming Arsenal to the Victoria Ground in blazing sunshine. The 15,000 crowd welcomed new signings George Berry, Mickey Thomas and Mark Chamberlain, but were not so generous to Lee Chapman with his new club. Chapman was booked inside five minutes but the real star was Chamberlain. The new recruit ran rings around the England left-back Kenny Sansom to create both of Stoke's goals, for Berry and Brendan O'Callaghan, as Stoke won 2-1.

SATURDAY 29TH AUGUST 1925

The previously-named Stoke became Stoke City and their first match with their new name was also the first game of the season, at home to Stockport County in the Second Division. A solid 3-0 win came thanks to two Joe Clennell goals and one from Bobby Archibald.

SATURDAY 29TH AUGUST 1981

Stoke beat Arsenal at Highbury on the opening day of the season thanks to a Lee Chapman goal. Richie Barker's first game in charge after replacing Alan Durban resulted in a rare win for the Potters in North London, one of only five in the league in 37 attempts. Stoke had shirt sponsors for the first time thanks to technology firm Ricoh.

SATURDAY 30TH AUGUST 1941

The opening game of the 1941/42 season saw Stoke welcome Everton to the Victoria Ground. The Potters were convincing winners in front of the 4,000 or so present. The 8-3 scoreline included a hat-trick for Tommy Sale. Sale scored more hat-tricks than anybody else in his Stoke career. His total of 28 includes 23 made during the war and 12 of the hat-tricks occurred in the 1941/42 season including a double hat-trick against Walsall.

TUESDAY 30TH AUGUST 1994

Stoke were level at 0-0 on 55 minutes when referee Pooley intervened in the match. After some trouble between the players the referee sent off City's Vince Overson and Wayne Biggins, but nobody from Reading. The nine-man Stoke side capitulated and the floodgates opened with Reading scoring four goals in the last half hour at Elm Park.

SATURDAY 30TH AUGUST 1997

The Britannia Stadium was finally ready to host league football, but not until Stanley Matthews unintentionally created a bad omen by missing the net from 12 yards during the opening celebrations. Richard Forsyth gave Stoke the lead but Swindon spoilt the party for the 23,000 present as they scored two late goals to take all three points.

SATURDAY 31st AUGUST 1929

C E Sutcliffe, league vice-president, opened the new covered Butler Street Stand which could hold 12,000. A gate of 16,569 attended the match to witness a 2-0 victory over Bradford City.

SATURDAY 31st AUGUST 1935

Bob McGrory's first game as Stoke manager is a victory at Elland Road. Joe Johnson netted two and Harry Davies one as Leeds could only muster one in reply.

SATURDAY 31st AUGUST 1957

Stoke set the pace at the top of the Second Division table by winning their first three matches. The 2-0 success at Leyton Orient came thanks to goals from Harry Oscroft and George 'Grace' Kelly.

TUESDAY 31st AUGUST 1993

Over twenty years after they last entered the competition, Stoke were again back in the Anglo-Italian Cup, hoping for a less volatile time. Their first match in their English qualification group was at Molineux where they earned a 3-3 draw with Wolves, Martin Carruthers scoring two.

THURSDAY 31st AUGUST 2006

As the transfer window closed, Stoke moved to sign Jamaican international Ricardo Fuller from Southampton on a three-year contract. The pacy and skilful forward put aside doubts about his knees and played a vital role in Stoke's promotion to the Premiership in 2007/08, finishing as joint top scorer for the season with Liam Lawrence on 15 league and cup goals.

WEDNESDAY 1st SEPTEMBER 1909

The first game Stoke ever played in the Southern League produced a handsome 11-0 victory over Welsh side Merthyr Tydfil. Billy Smith scored four and Arthur Griffiths also netted a hat-trick. Griffiths had two spells at Stoke sandwiching a time at Oldham Athletic after the club went out of business in 1908. The inside-right totalled 51 goals in 121 appearances for the Potters, before finally going to Wrexham.

SATURDAY 1st SEPTEMBER 1984

In what would turn out to be a rare moment of hope, Stoke elevated themselves to the dizzy heights of 17th with an early season victory over Sheffield Wednesday. Stoke's flu-ravaged side hung on for the win despite Paul Dyson seeing red for head butting Lee Chapman.

SATURDAY 2nd SEPTEMBER 1939

Stoke travelled to Ayresome Park to play Middlesbrough and came away with a point, after drawing 2-2, which left them ninth in the table after three matches. This was the last game before the league was cancelled for the war, with the three matches removed from the records, and it would be seven years until the next Football League match.

WEDNESDAY 2nd SEPTEMBER 1992

Mark Stein's goal at Valley Parade was not enough to prevent Bradford City winning 3-1. The defeat would be the Potters' last until February as they embarked on an unbeaten run of 25 games that would, in the end, see them promoted back to the First Division.

FRIDAY 3rd SEPTEMBER 1948

Jack Peart, who scored an incredible 41 goals in 47 games for Stoke, died in Paddington in London. He died whilst still in office as manager of Fulham, having been in charge at Craven Cottage for thirteen years.

MONDAY 3rd SEPTEMBER 1951

After completing his ban for leaving to play in Colombia, George Mountford came back to the Stoke team in a 1-1 draw at home to Fulham. John Malkin scored the City goal against the Cottagers.

MONDAY 4TH SEPTEMBER 1905

Two goals from Jack Hall and one from Teddy Holdcroft saw Stoke top the Division One table after a 3-0 victory against Blackburn Rovers. City stayed on top until the end of the month when they were overtaken by Sheffield Wednesday.

SATURDAY 4TH SEPTEMBER 1915

Joe Schofield's first match as Stoke City manager was a 3-1 success against Preston North End in the wartime football league, with the goals coming from Dicky Smith, Joey Jones and Bob Whittingham.

SATURDAY 4TH SEPTEMBER 1954

The goalless local derby in the Second Division against Port Vale drew a crowd of 46,990, which is the third highest for a league match at the Victoria Ground. Stoke have won 16 of the Football League encounters between the two sides, with 15 being drawn and Vale winning 13.

SATURDAY 5TH SEPTEMBER 1908

The newly formed Stoke club played its first game in the Birmingham and District League, with Alfred Barker taking charge for the first time. Aston Villa reserves were beaten 5-3 at the Victoria Ground in front of 12,000 fans. There was a brace apiece for Bert Myatt and Alf Owen, with 'Longton Billy' Davies grabbing the other. Davies scored a goal every two games before his career was ended through a knee injury aged just 23.

SATURDAY 5TH SEPTEMBER 1998

Brian Little unsurprisingly won the Manager of the Month award for steering Stoke to six wins in the first six games of the season. The latest, a two-goal victory over AFC Bournemouth, courtesy of Peter Thorne and Dean Crowe, made Stoke early-season favourites for the title.

MONDAY 6TH SEPTEMBER 1926

Stoke beat Wigan Borough 3-0 thanks to goals from Walter Bussey, Bobby Archibald and Charlie Wilson. The victory sent the Potters to the top of the Third Division (North) table after only four games, and this was a position they would maintain throughout the season.

WEDNESDAY 6TH SEPTEMBER 1972

As holders of the League Cup, Stoke started the defence of their crown at home to Second Division Sunderland. Progress to the third round was comfortable with two goals from Jimmy Greenhoff and one from Geoff Hurst in front of 16,706.

TUESDAY 6TH SEPTEMBER 1994

The 1-1 draw at home to Ancona in front of 3,330 was Joe Jordan's last game in charge as he was sacked shortly afterwards. It was not the Anglo-Italian Cup tie which lost him his job, but the one win in six at the start of the season and two successive 4-0 defeats, to Reading and Bolton Wanderers.

SATURDAY 7TH SEPTEMBER 1895

Stoke sat on top of the Football League for the first time ever after a 2-1 victory against Derby County, with Joe Schofield scoring both. Despite only two games having been played, Stoke were top by virtue of having a superior goal average to both Sunderland and Aston Villa. The Potters remained top for three weeks until being passed by Bolton Wanderers.

SATURDAY 8TH SEPTEMBER 1888

The historic first day of the inaugural Football League season saw Stoke host West Bromwich Albion. Goals from Joe Wilson and George Woodhall, both in the last six minutes, condemned Stoke to a 2-0 defeat in front of 4,524 spectators. The first secretary of the league, formed on 17th April, was the Stoke secretary Harry Lockett.

WEDNESDAY 8TH SEPTEMBER 1971

Stoke started their League Cup campaign away to Fourth Division Southport in the second round and came through 2-1 thanks to goals from John Ritchie and Jimmy Greenhoff. The road to Wembley started here.

TUESDAY 8TH SEPTEMBER 1998

City defender Chris Short collapsed at Craven Cottage and needed to be given oxygen to bring him round. On the pitch, Stoke slipped to their first defeat of the season thanks to a Rufus Brevett goal for Kevin Keegan's Fulham. City remained top.

WEDNESDAY 9TH SEPTEMBER 1970

During the goalless League Cup encounter with Millwall, Willie Stevenson broke his collarbone and received treatment from the Stoke physio Fred Street. Street set up a physiotherapy department at the club after being persuaded to enter football by his friend Bertie Mee. He remained at Stoke until Mee signed him for Arsenal, from City chairman Albert Henshall, for a fee of £5,000! Street went on to be the England physio for an astonishing 22 years.

WEDNESDAY 9TH SEPTEMBER 2000

Stefan Thordarson, Kyle Lightbourne and Graham Kavanagh scored as Stoke beat Peterborough United 3-0 at the Britannia Stadium to start a charge up the table. Just four days later there was another goal feast but this time Oxford United were the visitors and Stoke went one better with Bjarni Gudjonsson, James O'Connor, Marvin Robinson and Stefan Thordarson scoring in the 4-0 win.

SATURDAY 10TH SEPTEMBER 1898

The first win of the season came in the third game at the expense of Burnley. John Farrell, Harry Mellor, Joe Schofield and Jack Kennedy all got their names on the score sheet as Stoke finished up by winning 4-1.

SATURDAY 10TH SEPTEMBER 1958

Dennis Wilshaw grabbed two as Stoke won a thrilling game 4-3 at home to Scunthorpe United. A crowd of 17,824 were there to watch the Second Division clash as Johnny King and Peter Bullock netted Stoke's other goals. Don Ratcliffe played in midfield in this game and once again showed his versatility. Ratcliffe came through the ranks at Stoke and remained for 13 years, notching up 260 appearances.

SATURDAY 11TH SEPTEMBER 1937

An early season 8-1 hammering of Derby County lifted the Potters to top spot. Freddie Steele scored five of the goals and Jim Westland also scored a hat-trick. Aberdeen-born Westland, whose brother Doug also played in goal for Stoke, played in the Potteries for 11 years although the Second World War disrupted his career greatly.

SATURDAY 11TH SEPTEMBER 1982

Mickey Thomas scored his first goal for Stoke against Swansea City, smashing a free-kick past Dai Davies in a 4-1 win in the First Division. Thomas was described by Richie Barker as being irresponsible on the field and irresponsible off it!

MONDAY 12TH SEPTEMBER 1892

The game between Stoke and Aston Villa inspired a change in the rules. Villa were leading 1-0 with two minutes left when Stoke were awarded a penalty. Goalkeeper Bill Dunning kicked the ball out of the ground and by the time it was retrieved time was up and Stoke had lost. The rules were changed to allow time to be added on for a penalty kick.

WEDNESDAY 12TH SEPTEMBER 1962

Dennis Viollet scored four against Charlton Athletic as Stoke won 6-3. Viollet had been a prolific goalscorer for Manchester United before joining City. He scored a total of 179 goals in 293 outings in major competitions for the Old Trafford club before going on to score a further 66 times for Stoke.

SATURDAY 13TH SEPTEMBER 1890

Stoke started their first and only season in the Football Alliance with a 6-3 victory over Birmingham St George's, Charlie Baker scoring four as new manager Joseph Bradshaw got off to the perfect start.

SATURDAY 13TH SEPTEMBER 1941

Wrexham were on the receiving end of a 7-1 defeat at the hands of Stoke. The visitors' victory came thanks to two goals each for Tommy Sale and Frank Bowyer and one each for Alf Basnett, Edwin Blunt and Harry Brigham from the penalty spot.

WEDNESDAY 13TH SEPTEMBER 1972

As winners of the League Cup, Stoke earned a place in the Uefa Cup and their first tie in Europe was at home to the German side Kaiserslautern. Terry Conroy, Geoff Hurst and John Ritchie scored as Stoke ran out 3-1 winners, although it could have been more if not for goalkeeper Josef Elting.

SATURDAY 13TH SEPTEMBER 1980

Stoke suffered a 2-0 defeat at Highbury after setting out with a highly defensive mindset. When questioned about these tactics manager Alan Durban famously said: "If you want entertainment go and watch clowns".

SATURDAY 14TH SEPTEMBER 1889

Stoke suffered their worst ever league defeat, 10-0 at Deepdale at the hands of champions Preston North End.

MONDAY 14TH SEPTEMBER 1925

A Harry Sellars goal and a Tom Howe penalty were all Stoke had to show for their trip to Oldham Athletic, where the home side ran out 7-2 winners. The season would turn into a futile relegation struggle.

SATURDAY 14TH SEPTEMBER 1953

Harry Connor became the last amateur to play for Stoke City. In the early days all players had been amateurs, but the club had taken a decision to turn professional in 1885. Several amateur players had played for the club since that date, but Connor was the last. He made just four appearances for the club and scored two goals.

TUESDAY 14TH SEPTEMBER 2004

A crowd of 23,029 were at the Britannia Stadium to see Stoke go top of Division One. Jason De Vos gave Ipswich Town the lead but Wayne Thomas levelled before half-time. After the break the visitors again went ahead through Ian Westlake before Thomas grabbed his second. Ade Akinbiyi scored the winner with only five minutes to go.

SATURDAY 15TH SEPTEMBER 1894

Stoke travelled to Ewood Park to face Blackburn Rovers and were forced to make three changes to the team due to injury. The lack of first choice players showed and Blackburn rattled up six without reply.

SATURDAY 15TH SEPTEMBER 1951

A Stoke team shuffled due to injuries was soundly beaten 6-1 at home by Tottenham Hotspur. Harry Oscroft got the goal in front of the watching 27,000 at the Victoria Ground.

WEDNESDAY 16TH SEPTEMBER 1959

Lincoln City were swept aside in front of 13,453 at the Victoria Ground. Dennis Wilshaw helped himself to a hat-trick and two from Bill Bentley, and a Dickie Cunliffe strike, completed the scoring in the 6-1 win.

WEDNESDAY 16TH SEPTEMBER 1987

The central defensive partnership of George Berry and Steve Bould was renewed after Bould's back injury. The new solidness provided a platform and Steve Parkin scored to beat Reading at Elm Park. George Berry was a real fans' favourite who in his younger days had the most distinctive hairstyle of any footballer. At his testimonial game against Port Vale in 1990 he kissed the turf and spent the last hour of the match stood on the Boothen End.

SATURDAY 17TH SEPTEMBER 1898

A crowd of 8,000 at Bramall Lane witnessed a 1-1 draw thanks to a Willie Maxwell goal. Tom Holford made his debut at centre-half for Stoke in the match, although it was two years before he made the position his own. 'Dirty Tom' played 269 times for City scoring 33 goals before moving to Manchester City in 1908 as the club suffered great financial difficulties. He was rewarded with an England cap in the 4-0 win against Ireland in 1903.

SATURDAY 17TH SEPTEMBER 1983

Watford's visit to the Victoria Ground earned them three points as they won at a canter. The Boothen End called for Richie Barker to go long before John Barnes added Watford's fourth as the long-ball system simply did not work for the Potters. Stoke were left in 20th place and in serious trouble after five defeats in the first six games.

TUESDAY 17TH SEPTEMBER 1991

On loan from Oxford United, Mark Stein made his debut away at Hartlepool United. He did not make it onto the score sheet, but Wayne Biggins did grab two and John Butler the other as the Potters won 3-2 at Victoria Park.

WEDNESDAY 18TH SEPTEMBER 1974

Denis Smith scored late on to earn a 1-1 draw in the Uefa Cup first round first leg against Ajax. A crowd of 37,398 at the Victoria Ground had seen the Dutch side take the lead through Ruud Krol just before half time. The Potters were outplayed by an Ajax team including Johnny Rep, Arie Haan and Arnold Muhren, leaving an uphill task for the second leg in the Stadion de Meer.

WEDNESDAY 18TH SEPTEMBER 1985

Stoke City caused an upset by beating First Division Coventry City 3-0 in the first round of the new Full Members' Cup in front of 3,516 fans.

SATURDAY 19TH SEPTEMBER 1936

Stoke thrashed Middlesbrough 6-2 thanks to a Freddie Steele hat-trick, two from Joe Johnson and one from Stanley Matthews. The starting XI had seen William Moore come in for his debut in place of Arthur Tutin. This brought to an end a run of 36 consecutive matches when Stoke had fielded the same back line of Norman Wilkinson, Bill Winstanley, Charlie Scrimshaw, Arthur Tutin, Arthur Turner and Frankie Soo.

SATURDAY 19TH SEPTEMBER 1992

Table-topping West Bromwich Albion led twice in this see-saw match but lost 4-3 thanks to Ian Cranson's late header which went in off the bar.

SUNDAY 19TH SEPTEMBER 1993

The first live televised league match to involve Stoke City took place at the City Ground in Nottingham, although it did not stop more than 3,000 Stoke supporters attending the match. City raced into a three-goal lead before Forest woke up and clawed it back to 3-2. Stoke held on for all three points.

WEDNESDAY 20TH SEPTEMBER 1933

Dennis Viollet, who survived the Munich air disaster, was born in Manchester. After scoring a goal every two games at Old Trafford he was mysteriously allowed to leave for Stoke and continued to score goals for the Potters, totalling 66 in his five years at the Victoria Ground.

FRIDAY 20TH SEPTEMBER 1946

In Cardiff, South Wales, long-serving Stoke midfielder John Mahoney was born to a rugby-playing father. Mahoney played for City for more than a decade before moving to Middlesbrough for £90,000 in 1977. He amassed 51 Welsh caps during his career before retiring in 1984.

SUNDAY 20TH SEPTEMBER 1953

Alan Dodd, who played over 400 games for Stoke in two spells, was born in the Potteries. 'Doddy' also played for Wolves, and twice for Port Vale.

THURSDAY 21ST SEPTEMBER 1876

William Sturrock Maxwell, Stoke's high scoring inside-left, was born in Arbroath. He was employed as a solicitor's clerk and moved to City from Heart of Midlothian as he had taken up a job in Stoke.

SATURDAY 21ST SEPTEMBER 1895

Tom Hyslop scored a hat-trick to beat West Bromwich Albion 3-1 and extend Stoke's winning streak to nine matches, a club record. The run, ironically, started against the Albion too.

MONDAY 21ST SEPTEMBER 1953

After signing from Crewe Alexandra for £8,000, Johnny King made his Stoke City debut at Millmoor. The forward did not score in the 2-2 draw against Rotherham United, but Bill Finney and Johnny Malkin did.

SATURDAY 22ND SEPTEMBER 1945

With centre-half Neil Franklin away on international duty with England, Newcastle United thumped Stoke City 9-1 at St James' Park in front of 45,000. Stand-in centre-half, Stuart Cowden, was given a torrid time by Albert Stubbins who scored five times in the match.

SATURDAY 22ND SEPTEMBER 1956

There were six different goalscorers in Stoke's 7-1 victory over Leyton Orient: Bobby Cairns, Tim Coleman, George Kelly, Johnny King, Frank Bowyer and Harry Oscroft, who hit two. The match at the Victoria Ground was watched by 19,957. During the 1956/57 season Stoke City scored eight once, seven once and six twice, with Tim Coleman scoring 12 in just those four games.

MONDAY 22ND SEPTEMBER 1969

A disappointing crowd of 23,000 turned out for the friendly visit of Brazilian side Santos, and the legendary Pelé, who scored twice in his side's 3-2 win. City were leading at half-time through John Ritchie and Jimmy Greenhoff, but it could have been 3-1 if the referee had not blown for the interval just as Denis Smith's header flew past Brazilian keeper Gilmar. Early in the second half Edu equalised before Pelé scored a wonderful winner ten minutes from time.

WEDNESDAY 22ND SEPTEMBER 1993

The prize for defeating Mansfield Town in the first round of the Coca-Cola Cup was a two-legged tie against champions Manchester United. The first leg saw a wonderful performance by Stoke and in particular Mark Stein who scored two wonderful goals to send the Boothen End wild and give the Potters the edge going in to the second leg at Old Trafford.

SATURDAY 23RD SEPTEMBER 1916

Two goals from Arthur Bridgett were mere consolation as Stoke were thumped 9-2 by Bolton Wanderers in the Lancashire Section Primary Competition of war football.

WEDNESDAY 23RD SEPTEMBER 1970

Denis Smith earned representative honours when he played for the Football League against the Irish League at Norwich City's Carrow Road.

SATURDAY 23RD SEPTEMBER 1989

The Victoria Ground was a 27,032 sell-out for the first Potteries derby in 32 years. Stoke fell behind to John Rudge's Vale side through former City trainee Robbie Earle, but the Potters earned a draw thanks to Leigh Palin's deflected shot.

MONDAY 24TH SEPTEMBER 1883

A crowd of around 3,000 turned up to witness the first match at the newly named Victoria Ground, a 1-1 draw against Great Lever. The game also saw Stoke adopt a new kit of red and white striped shirts and white shorts. They had previously played in blue and black striped shirts with white shorts, and then in claret shirts with white shorts.

TUESDAY 24TH SEPTEMBER 1974

Ipswich scored three in 16 minutes to round off a rotten night for the Potters. Stoke had Alan Dodd sent off and John Ritchie carried off in the 3-1 defeat. With the scores level at 0-0, Kevin Beattie's tackle caused a double leg fracture to Ritchie which ended his league career, although he did spend some time with Stafford Rangers.

SATURDAY 25TH SEPTEMBER 1926

During Stoke's Division Three (North) championship-winning season Charlie Wilson scored five in a 7-0 drubbing of Ashington. This was the first occasion any Stoke player had scored five goals in a Football League fixture.

SATURDAY 25TH SEPTEMBER 1982

With the score 2-1 in Stoke's favour, Peter Fox was sent off for handling outside the penalty area, and Paul Bracewell initially took his place. Luton Town fought back to lead 4-3 until Brendan O'Callaghan levelled in the 84th minute. David Moss had a last-minute penalty against second stand-in keeper Derek Parkin, but hit the post. The result, an incredible 4-4 draw.

WEDNESDAY 25TH SEPTEMBER 1991

Lou Macari's men took a following of 6,000 to Anfield in the League Cup first round and in the 88th minute Tony Kelly nutmegged Bruce Grobbelaar to ensure the scores were level at 2-2 for the second leg.

SATURDAY 26TH SEPTEMBER 1868

An issue of *The Field* magazine made what appears to be the first reference to a club formed to play football in Stoke-on-Trent. Debate has raged about the origins of the club and whether they were founded in 1863, as long believed, or in 1868 as now seems likely.

SATURDAY 26TH SEPTEMBER 1914

The 11-0 FA Cup preliminary round victory against Stourbridge was the club's biggest FA Cup win and their only ever game at this stage of the competition. Arty Watkin scored five, Fred McCarthy three, Billy Herbert two and Henry Hargreaves one as Southern League Stoke headed to the first qualifying round.

SATURDAY 26TH SEPTEMBER 1925

Stoke beat Middlesbrough 4-0 at the Victoria Ground in front of 9,617 fans. Bobby Archibald scored one of the goals with George Paterson scoring a hat-trick on his league debut. The Scot suffered a bad leg injury which restricted him to only six more appearances for Stoke.

SATURDAY 26TH SEPTEMBER 1970

Eventual double winners Arsenal visited Stoke in front of the *Match of the Day* cameras as City pulled off an astonishing result. Goals from Alan Bloor, Jimmy Greenhoff, two from John Ritchie and a Terry Conroy strike, which won 'Goal of the Month', resulted in a 5-0 drubbing for the champions-to-be.

TUESDAY 26TH SEPTEMBER 2000

A real nip and tuck cup tie at The Valley was settled by away goals in Stoke's favour, despite Premiership Charlton Athletic winning 4-3 on the night to give an aggregate score of 5-5. The defining moment was a stunning strike from Stefan Thordarson from the left wing.

SATURDAY 27TH SEPTEMBER 1952

George Mountford made his fourth and last appearance of the season in the 2-0 reverse at Cardiff. New boss Frank Taylor did not take too long to move him on to Queens Park Rangers for a fee of £4,000.

WEDNESDAY 27TH SEPTEMBER 1972

Stoke City's first foray into European football ended in tears as Kaiserslautern overturned a 3-1 first leg deficit with a 4-0 win in Germany. At 3-0 down after just over an hour, Tony Waddington sent on John Ritchie to grab a vital goal, but he was sent off after only nine seconds for hitting Yugoslav international Idriz Hosic.

SATURDAY 28TH SEPTEMBER 1895

A crowd of 6,000 saw Stoke lose 1-0 at Sheffield United, a defeat which ended their record winning streak of nine games.

SATURDAY 28TH SEPTEMBER 1957

The 1-0 defeat at Leeds Road to Huddersfield Town marked the end of the career of Frank Mountford after 18 years as a pro with Stoke.

SATURDAY 29TH SEPTEMBER 1934

Stanley Matthews became the first Stoke player for over 30 years to appear in a full international for England. Matthews scored from the right wing as Wales were beaten 4-0 in Cardiff.

WEDNESDAY 29TH SEPTEMBER 1971

The Anglo-Scottish Cup again drew Stoke against Motherwell and after a 1-0 win at Fir Park, City won the second leg convincingly 4-1 thanks to a brace from John Ritchie and a goal apiece for Jimmy Greenhoff and Sean Haslegrave. The cup run was short-lived as Derby County proved too strong in the next round.

THURSDAY 30TH SEPTEMBER 1909

The impressive start to the Southern League season of 1909/10 continued with an 8-1 thumping of Ton Pentre hot on the heels of the 11-0 victory over Merthyr. Arthur Griffiths again scored a hat-trick as Stoke eased past the Welsh opposition.

WEDNESDAY 30TH SEPTEMBER 1970

Having entered the Anglo-Scottish Cup for the first time, Stoke were drawn against Motherwell. After the two legs scores were level at 2-2 – City were about to face their first ever penalty shoot-out. The penalties were lost 4-3 and this started a trend. Stoke have been involved in 12 penalty shoot-outs in competitive matches, only winning two.

SATURDAY 1st OCTOBER 1949

A crowd of 49,903 were at St James' Park to see Newcastle United beat Stoke 4-1. The match marked a return to the team for Billy Mould, the versatile defender who represented City for 16 years.

SATURDAY 1st OCTOBER 1983

Top-of-the-table West Ham United were well beaten at the Victoria Ground by 3-1. Stoke's goals came from Mickey Thomas, Mark Chamberlain and a Dave McAughtrie overhead kick!

TUESDAY 2nd OCTOBER 1973

The Texaco Cup match against Birmingham City went to penalties after two goalless draws, and Stoke lost the shoot-out 3-1.

WEDNESDAY 2nd OCTOBER 1974

Piet Schrijvers was the hero for Ajax as Stoke were knocked out of the Uefa Cup on away goals in the first round. A 1-1 draw in the Potteries put the onus on Stoke to score first and they took the game to the Dutch from the off. Ajax held on for a 0-0 draw as Jimmy Robertson's last-minute shot from six yards was deflected over by Schrijvers' left boot.

SUNDAY 2nd OCTOBER 1994

Lou Macari's return as manager was widely rejoiced as Stoke thumped West Bromwich Albion 4-1 in front of the ITV cameras. Martin Carruthers, with two, and strikes from Ray Wallace and Paul Peschisolido, helped to sink Albion at the Victoria Ground in front of 14,203 fans.

SATURDAY 3rd OCTOBER 1891

Stoke hit the bottom of the Football League after losing 9-3 at Darwen. As league rules stated all teams had to play in different strips, and as Sunderland already had red and white stripes, Stoke played the 1891/92 league season in black and amber striped shirts.

TUESDAY 3rd OCTOBER 1978

In the League Cup third round tie at Northampton Town, Stoke gave a debut to Potteries-born striker Adrian Heath. 'Inchy' set up the crucial third goal for Howard Kendall as Stoke progressed to the next round and a date at Charlton Athletic.

SATURDAY 4TH OCTOBER 1958

The visit of Bristol Rovers ended in a draw with Kenny Thompson and Frank Bowyer netting for Stoke. The match was the last played for City by Neville Coleman who moved to Crewe Alexandra.

WEDNESDAY 4TH OCTOBER 1995

Paul Peschisolido scored a 75th-minute winner at Stamford Bridge as Stoke progressed to the third round of the League Cup. Ex-Potter Mark Stein missed a sitter at the death for Glenn Hoddle's team.

WEDNESDAY 5TH OCTOBER 1887

Stoke hosted Burslem Port Vale for the first competitive Potteries derby. The FA Cup tie was won 1-0 thanks to George Lawton's strike, and Stoke were in the second round.

SATURDAY 5TH OCTOBER 1901

Nottingham Forest were the visitors to the Victoria Ground in front of an 8,000 crowd. The match ended 1-1 with Fred Johnson scoring for the Potters. Johnson was an outside-right who spent eight years at Stoke, his only professional club. Representative honours came his way as he played for the English League against the Irish League in 1903. Johnson played 196 times for the club and notched 20 goals. He was rewarded with a testimonial game against the famous amateur side, Corinthians, during 1901, which ended 3-3.

SATURDAY 5TH OCTOBER2002

A 1-1 draw at the Britannia Stadium against Crystal Palace, with Chris Iwelumo netting, was the last match in charge for Steve Cotterill before he walked out on the club to become Howard Wilkinson's assistant at Sunderland.

SATURDAY 6TH OCTOBER 1888

Borrowed from the home team at Preston North End, William Smalley and Archie Dempsey played their only games for Stoke. Two of the Stoke players had missed the train to the match and so the pair were borrowed to make up the numbers. Neither of the players ever made Preston's first team, and they made little impact in this match as Stoke lost 7-0 to the eventual champions.

SATURDAY 6TH OCTOBER 1956

Stoke beat Rotherham United 6-0 at home with the goals coming from Johnny King, Tim Coleman with two, and one each for Harry Oscroft and Frank Bowyer. The Second Division fixture was seen by 21,589 at the Victoria Ground.

WEDNESDAY 6TH OCTOBER 1971

Stoke were lucky to come away from Second Division Oxford United with a replay in the third round of the League Cup. United were on top throughout the match at the Manor Ground. Jimmy Greenhoff scored early on after a mistake by the home keeper as Stoke claimed a 1-1 draw.

WEDNESDAY 6TH OCTOBER 1993

A plucky display at Old Trafford was not enough as United overcame a 2-1 first leg deficit to progress to the third round of the League Cup. A late Brian McClair goal sealed a 3-2 aggregate win for United, much to the disappointment of the 9,000-strong Stoke following.

MONDAY 7TH OCTOBER 1889

On the way back from Wolverhampton the train carrying the Stoke players was involved in an accident at Stafford station. The injuries sustained put Jack Eccles out of action for a month.

SATURDAY 7TH OCTOBER 1916

Amateur goalkeeper Dr Leigh Richmond Roose was killed in action serving in France with the 9th Royal Fusiliers. Roose played 24 times for Wales and for a number of clubs including Sunderland, Woolwich Arsenal, Celtic, Aston Villa, Everton, Port Vale and two spells at Stoke.

MONDAY 8TH OCTOBER 1928

Legendary Stoke full-back Alf Underwood died in Stoke-on-Trent. He had been ill for 20 years and Stoke manager Denny Austerberry had set up a fund to prevent him from becoming destitute due to the illness.

SATURDAY 9TH OCTOBER 1926

A crowd of just under 9,000 turned out for the visit of Wrexham to the Victoria Ground. Stoke City kept themselves on top of the Third Division (North) thanks to goals from Harry Davies and Charlie Wilson.

WEDNESDAY 9TH OCTOBER 1991

Two goals from Wayne Biggins set up a tense finish at the Victoria Ground but Liverpool held on for a 5-4 aggregate win. The League Cup second round tie was watched by a crowd of 22,335. 'Bertie' Biggins was a real crowd favourite who scored 61 goals in his two spells at the club.

WEDNESDAY 10TH OCTOBER 1888

Stoke paid the penalty for entering their reserve side, the 'Swifts', into the FA Cup qualifying round. They were beaten 2-1 at home by Warwick County who later went out to Burton Wanderers.

SATURDAY 10TH OCTOBER 1908

Stoke hosted Wellington Town in the Birmingham League and a Vic Horrocks hat-trick helped them on their way to a 7-0 win in front of 5,000 at the 'Vic'.

SATURDAY 10TH OCTOBER 1931

Looking for a return to the First Division for the first time since 1922/23, Stoke went to the top of the table after a 1-0 win against Wolves. Bobby Liddle scored the goal in front of 30,000 at Molineux. Liddle gave a total of 25 years' service to Stoke City after signing as a professional in 1928, to being the club's trainer under Bob McGrory. Including wartime football, he made a total of 466 appearances for the club scoring 92 goals.

WEDNESDAY 10TH OCTOBER 1956

After the installation of floodlights at the Victoria Ground, 38,729 spectators turned up to see the first match in which they were used, a local Division Two derby against Port Vale. The home team won 3-1 thanks to two goals from Tim Coleman and one from George Kelly.

THURSDAY 10TH OCTOBER 2002

Only five months into his managerial post at Stoke, Steve Cotterill quit and became Howard Wilkinson's assistant at Sunderland. The manner of his departure left a bitter taste, both with his employers and the fans, and resulted in a long compensation battle with the Black Cats.

SATURDAY 11TH OCTOBER 1884

Glasgow club Queen's Park, on their way to the FA Cup Final, were left with a walkover to the next round after Stoke withdrew from the first qualifying round as they could not afford to travel to the match at Hampden Park in Scotland!

SATURDAY 11TH OCTOBER 1980

Alan Durban finally got his man as Iain Munro arrived from St Mirren having recovered from injury, and straight away Stoke pulled off an impressive victory at The Dell. Charlie George put Southampton ahead from the penalty spot but City came back in the second half to win through Munro and left-back Peter Hampton.

SATURDAY 12TH OCTOBER 1918

During the final season of wartime football, Stoke travelled to Port Vale for a local derby. Bob Whittingham, who would join Port Vale just six months later, scored four as Stoke won convincingly 8-1.

SATURDAY 12TH OCTOBER 1929

Wilf Kirkham and Charlie Wilson scored the goals as Stoke drew 2-2 at home to Reading in the Second Division. Wilson's strike was his 100th for the club – the first player to achieve this feat.

FRIDAY 12TH OCTOBER 2007

Mamady Sidibe, Stoke's Malian international striker, was hurt in a riot by Togo fans after Mali had beaten Togo 2-0 to qualify for the African Cup of Nations. Sidibe received severe arm injuries after being dragged through a broken window, and he nearly quit international football as a result.

SATURDAY 13TH OCTOBER 1906

It took until the ninth game of the season before Stoke registered their first victory, 2-1 at home to Derby County.

SATURDAY 13TH OCTOBER 1990

Tony Ellis scored two goals to move Stoke up to third place in Division Three. Alan Ball's side had made a good start to life in the lower divisions, although second-from-bottom Fulham forced a fantastic string of saves from Peter Fox in the 2-1 win.

MONDAY 14TH OCTOBER 1968

Young goalkeeper Paul Shardlow collapsed and died after a heart attack during a training session. Aged only 25, Stone-born Shardlow had made four first-team appearances for the club he joined from Northwich Victoria in 1966.

SATURDAY 14TH OCTOBER 2006

New loan signings Rory Delap, Salif Diao and Lee Hendrie made their mark during a fantastic 4-0 win at Elland Road. Stoke's first away win against struggling Leeds United for 25 years saw goals from Hendrie, Danny Higginbotham, Andy Griffin and Ricardo Fuller.

SATURDAY 15TH OCTOBER 1966

A Victoria Ground crowd of 25,554 saw Stoke head to the top of Division One, by a single point, after a 3-2 victory over Southampton. Peter Dobing, John Ritchie and Calvin Palmer scored Stoke's goals. Dobing would end the season as top scorer for the club with 19, from Harry Burrows on 17.

WEDNESDAY 15TH OCTOBER 1997

Premiership Leeds United visited the Britannia Stadium for the League Cup third round tie which went to extra time after a Graham Kavanagh penalty and a Harry Kewell equaliser. The Potters succumbed in extra time after two Rod Wallace goals against Chic Bates' tiring team.

SATURDAY 16TH OCTOBER 1971

Despite Gordon Banks playing with an injured knee, Stoke beat Coventry City 1-0 at The Victoria Ground in front of 20,040. The winner came in the 82nd minute from Denis Smith's head after a corner from Terry Conroy.

WEDNESDAY 16TH OCTOBER 1996

The hold Stoke had over West Bromwich Albion was in evidence again as Ray Wallace and Richard Forsyth scored to take three points from the Hawthorns, in front of 16,501 fans.

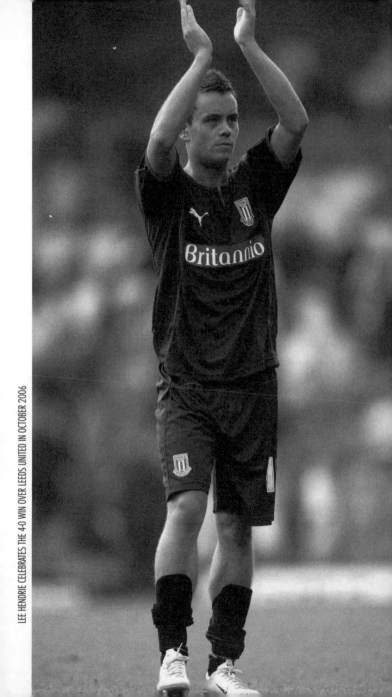

SATURDAY 17TH OCTOBER 1868

The newly-formed Stoke Ramblers club played its first game at the Victoria Cricket Club Ground versus Mr E W May's XV, resulting in a 1-1 draw. The first goal for the club was scored by Henry John Almond who was captain for the match and is the man credited with being the founder of the club. Former Charterhouse School pupil Almond moved to South America and became a civil engineer.

WEDNESDAY 17TH OCTOBER 1984

Mark Chamberlain became the last Stoke player to represent England when he came on as a sub for Bryan Robson in the World Cup qualifier against Finland at Wembley. Chamberlain's eighth cap came during a 5-0 win in front of 47,234.

TUESDAY 17TH OCTOBER 1989

West Bromwich Albion visited the Victoria Ground and Stoke won 2-1 in front of 11,991. The goals from Gary Hackett and Wayne Biggins ended the club's record run of 17 games without a win.

MONDAY 18TH OCTOBER 1909

Amos Baddeley scored four of Stoke's five goals against Brierley Hill Alliance in the Birmingham League Cup. The hat-trick was one of Baddeley's three for the season on his way to a career-best 29 goals. Of the four members of the Baddeley family to play for Stoke, Amos scored the most goals, totalling 56. He left Stoke for Blackpool when the club folded in 1908.

SATURDAY 18TH OCTOBER 1919

The Victory International at the Victoria Ground against Wales had a special significance for the locals. Stoke players Bob Whittingham and Charlie Parker both played, with Whittingham getting a goal.

TUESDAY 18TH OCTOBER 1960

Stoke opted to enter the inaugural Football League Cup competition and their first tie was in the second round, when they were drawn away to Doncaster Rovers. A full-strength Potters side went down 3-1 at Belle Vue to the Division Four outfit, who were defeated 7-0 by Chelsea in the next round.

WEDNESDAY 18TH OCTOBER 1961

Fourteen years after departing for Blackpool, Stanley Matthews rejoined Stoke for £3,000. Stan, now 46-years-old, signed live on BBC's *Sportsview* programme. Tony Waddington's masterstroke would ignite the imagination of the Potteries people, leading to increased attendances, a renewed belief in the team, and ultimately promotion back to the First Division the following year. Matthews would play 66 games in his second spell at the club, scoring five goals.

MONDAY 18TH OCTOBER 1971

Stoke won the League Cup third round replay against Oxford United to book a tie with Manchester United in round four. The 2-0 scoreline was slightly flattering to City who won thanks to John Ritchie and a late Sean Haslegrave strike at the Victoria Ground.

SATURDAY 19TH OCTOBER 1918

Fresh from beating Port Vale 8-1, Stoke hosted Blackburn Rovers and scored seven without reply. Arthur Lockett scored a hat-trick in the game as a guest player. He had previously played for Stoke from 1900 to 1903 before moving to Aston Villa, shortly after winning his only England cap. In the 1918/19 season Lockett guested 12 times.

TUESDAY 19TH OCTOBER 1937

Scottish giants Glasgow Rangers provided the opposition for a benefit game in aid of the Holditch Colliery disaster, which occurred when the mine near to Chesterton lost 30 men in an explosion during July. The Rangers team for the 0-0 draw included legendary players such as Jerry Dawson, Jimmy Simpson and Jimmy Smith.

WEDNESDAY 20TH OCTOBER 1920

Bob Whittingham's benefit match took place between a combined Stoke/Port Vale XI and the League Stars.

SATURDAY 20TH OCTOBER 1951

A 2-0 victory against Wolves completed an incredible turnaround for City. After drawing one and losing ten of the first 11 games, Stoke then won four in a row to lift themselves out of the First Division drop zone. The victory came courtesy of a Harry Oscroft strike in front of 43,205 fans.

TUESDAY 20TH OCTOBER 1987

Mick Mills made his last appearance as player-manager at Stoke before hanging up his boots and concentrating on his managerial role. Mills, who at 38 years and 289 days of age was the third-oldest player to represent Stoke since the war, had played in 44 matches since arriving in 1985.

THURSDAY 21ST OCTOBER 1943

Skegness was the location for the birth of Calvin Palmer. The midfielder/full-back played nearly 200 games for the club, but missed out on the tour to America to play as the Cleveland Stokers as he had an altercation with Maurice Setters prior to departure.

SATURDAY 21ST OCTOBER 1972

Stoke lost 2-1 at Anfield in what turned out to be Gordon Banks' last game for the club. The result was disputed. In the last minute, the referee played an advantage and then later brought it back for a free-kick anyway, which Ian Callaghan scored from.

SUNDAY 22ND OCTOBER 1972

Returning home from treatment at the Victoria Ground, Stoke and England goalkeeper Gordon Banks was involved in a car accident resulting in career-ending eye injuries.

TUESDAY 22ND OCTOBER 1974

The second replay of this third round League Cup tie was nowhere near as close as the previous two encounters. Stoke took a 6-0 lead before allowing two late consolations in front of over 26,000 at the Victoria Ground. The club's biggest League Cup victory included two goals for Geoff Hurst and own goals from both Ron Harris and Mickey Droy.

SATURDAY 23RD OCTOBER 1965

Bill Asprey played his last game for Stoke, replacing Calvin Palmer in the starting XI for the 2-1 defeat to Leeds United at Elland Road.

SATURDAY 23RD OCTOBER 1993

The last game of Lou Macari's first spell as Stoke manager ended with a point each at Molineux against Wolves, but the home side missed a penalty. Macari left Stoke in 14th place.

WEDNESDAY 23RD OCTOBER 1996

Arsene Wenger's Arsenal were severely tested in the Coca-Cola Cup at the Victoria Ground as Mike Sheron gave Stoke a first-half lead. The Gunners equalised late on through Ian Wright, although there was a hint of handball.

MONDAY 24TH OCTOBER 1910

Kettering Town were on the receiving end of an 8-1 beating in the Southern League. Jack Peart bagged a hat-trick, Jackie Brown scored two, and there was one each for George Turner, Billy Smith and Amos Baddeley.

SATURDAY 24TH OCTOBER 1925

For the second time in the season Stoke conceded seven, this time at Derby in front of 15,000 fans. The 7-3 scoreline helped to keep the Potters in the mire at the foot of the table.

SATURDAY 24TH OCTOBER 1992

A capacity crowd of 24,459 packed into the Victoria Ground for the Potteries derby, with Nigel Gleghorn making his City debut. Vale took the lead but Stoke equalised immediately through Ian Cranson. There was controversy as Mark Stein was brought down by Vale keeper Paul Musselwhite for a penalty with only four minutes remaining. The visiting players protested strongly but Stein got up to bury the spot-kick and Stoke held on to win.

SUNDAY 25TH OCTOBER 1931

Future Burnley, Stoke and Northern Ireland midfielder Jimmy McIlroy was born in Belfast. After nearly 500 games for Burnley he joined Tony Waddington's increasingly exciting Stoke team in March 1963, just in time to help Stoke to promotion. After retiring as a player he came back to City as a coach from 1968 until 1970. He was later manager of Bolton Wanderers for only 18 days in 1970.

WEDNESDAY 25TH OCTOBER 1995

Kevin Keegan's Newcastle United carved through City, with a helping hand from referee Ashby, who sent off Stoke's Ian Clarkson after two pieces of theatrics from David Ginola. The Premiership leaders were comfortable 4-0 winners in this Coca-Cola Cup third round tie.

THURSDAY 26TH OCTOBER 1905

Prolific scorer Joe Mawson was born at Brandon Colliery in County Durham. He followed his family's footsteps by going down the pit, before turning to professional football.

TUESDAY 26TH OCTOBER 1971

The first part of an epic Cup tie unfolded at Old Trafford as Stoke took the lead thanks to a John Ritchie goal. Alan Gowling scored late on to force a replay. The League Cup fourth round tie had been played in front of over 47,000 fans.

SATURDAY 27TH OCTOBER 1934

A 2-0 win at Stamford Bridge was clinched by a Tommy Sale brace. The victory at Chelsea lifted Stoke to the top of the First Division for the first time in 29 years.

TUESDAY 27TH OCTOBER 1987

Stoke beat First Division Norwich City 2-1 at the Victoria Ground – Gerry Daly and Brian Talbot scoring – to earn themselves a League Cup third round tie at home to Arsenal.

SATURDAY 28TH OCTOBER 1961

At 46-years-old, Stanley Matthews made his second debut for his hometown club. A crowd of 35,974 packed into the Victoria Ground – over 27,000 more than for the previous home game – to witness the match against Huddersfield Town. Matthews played well against future World Cup winner Ray Wilson, and Stoke ran out 3-0 winners thanks to a brace from Tommy Thompson and one from Jimmy Adam. The return of crowd favourite Matthews led a revival that would see City promoted.

WEDNESDAY 28TH OCTOBER 1981

Paired against Manchester City in the League Cup second round for the second year, City forced the tie to penalties after scoring two in the last ten minutes of normal time through Lee Chapman and Ray Evans. Stoke lost the shoot-out 9-8 after Peter Griffths' shot was saved by Joe Corrigan.

SATURDAY 29TH OCTOBER 1932

Stoke City defeated Notts County at Meadow Lane to go three points clear at the top of the Second Division table. Joe Mawson with two, and Bobby Liddle and Joe Johnson with one each, were the scorers in a 4-3 victory.

SATURDAY 30TH OCTOBER 1886

In the FA Cup qualifying round, Stoke recorded their best ever cup victory with a 10-1 thrashing of Caernarvon Wanderers. Alf Edge helped himself to five goals, Ted Bennett bagged three and Tommy Clare two.

SATURDAY 30TH OCTOBER 1909

Amos Baddeley scored after only eight seconds against West Bromwich Albion reserves in the Birmingham League at the Victoria Ground, making it possibly the fastest goal ever scored by a Stoke player. Despite the great start Stoke went on to lose the match 3-1.

SATURDAY 30TH OCTOBER 1993

After losing manager Lou Macari to Celtic and top scorer Mark Stein to Chelsea, caretaker manager Chic Bates saw his Stoke team involved in an incredible game at the 'Vic'. Barnsley went two up in seven minutes. Two own goals in two minutes restored parity before Barnsley scored just before the break for 3-2. Three goals in 15 minutes gave Stoke a 5-3 lead then Barnsley scored with five minutes left to set up a dramatic finish. The Potters hung on to win 5-4.

SATURDAY 31ST OCTOBER 1885

Crewe Alexandra forced a replay in the FA Cup against Harry Lockett's Stoke team, with the Potters goals coming from Jimmy Sayer and George Shutt.

SATURDAY 31ST OCTOBER 1908

Having resigned from the Football League, the newly-reformed Stoke FC had entered the Birmingham and District League for 1908/09. West Bromwich Albion reserves hammered them 8-1 in front of a crowd of 5,000. Harry Davies netted the Stoke goal.

WEDNESDAY 1st NOVEMBER 2000

Rikki Dadason came off the bench on his debut to score with a last-gasp header, earning a fourth round League Cup spot versus Liverpool. The other goals in the 3-2 win over Barnsley came from manager's son Bjarni Gudjonsson.

THURSDAY 1st NOVEMBER 2002

Tony Pulis is named as new manager, despite being the board's second choice, after Steve Cotterill had quit for Sunderland. The job was taken by George Burley. However, after watching the team lose at home to Watford the night before, Burley did not turn up for the already arranged press conference, much to Stoke's embarrassment.

SATURDAY 2nd NOVEMBER 1889

Stoke went down 8-0 at Everton to leave them with only one win from the first eight games of the season.

TUESDAY 2nd NOVEMBER 1999

The club announced it was being taken over by an Icelandic consortium. The deal to buy Stoke City from Peter Coates and Keith Humphreys would be finalised on 15th November and future plans would be outlined on this date. Magnus Kristinsson, the financial clout behind the consortium, said he planned to turn Stoke into a "very big club".

SATURDAY 2nd NOVEMBER 2002

Dave Kevan was effectively in charge of team selection for Tony Pulis' first game in charge after being caretaker manager. Walsall won 4-2 at the Bescot Stadium where the Stoke goals were scored by Andy Cooke and Chris Greenacre.

WEDNESDAY 2nd NOVEMBER 2005

During the 2-1 away victory at Coventry City – courtesy of goals from Paul Gallagher and Gerry Taggart – a row broke out which dominated the season. Manager Johan Boskamp threatened to resign if director of football John Rudge did not go, after Boskamp had fallen out with both Rudge and assistant manager Jan De Koning over a note passed between them. Rudge was sent on leave later until Boskamp departed in the summer.

SATURDAY 3RD NOVEMBER 1984

Ronnie Whelan scored in the 86th minute to defeat City at the Victoria Ground. Stoke put up a strong performance against Liverpool with new on-loan goalkeeper Joe Corrigan making his debut due to Peter Fox's back injury. The defeat left the Potters at the foot of the table, a position they would not leave again all season.

WEDNESDAY 3RD NOVEMBER 1999

Stoke were all over Notts County at Meadow Lane, but somehow lost 1-0. The City midfield looked a class above their Magpie counterparts with Kevin Keen raiding down the wing. The former West Ham United man spent six years with the Pottters, appearing in 203 games for the club before moving to Macclesfield Town.

SATURDAY 4TH NOVEMBER 1933

The half-back line dubbed as the 'Arsenal of the North' made its first appearance in a 6-1 defeat at Middlesbrough. Debutants Arthur Tutin and Hong Yi 'Frankie' Soo lined up alongside the more established Arthur Turner, and they went on to form one of the most famous partnerships in the club's history. Frankie Soo also became the first player of Chinese descent to appear in the league.

SATURDAY 4TH NOVEMBER 1989

Dave Bamber scored his first goal in ten matches, but it came at the wrong end as Stoke were thrashed 6-0 at Swindon Town. Ossie Ardiles' side were too good for City who slipped to second from bottom. Inevitably, this turned out to be Mick Mills' last game as Stoke manager.

SATURDAY 5TH NOVEMBER 1910

Having entered both the Birmingham League and the Southern League, the fixture lists dictated that Stoke had to field two first-team sides on the same day. This did not cause too many problems as Kidderminster Harriers could only take a point after a 2-2 draw in the Birmingham League and Chesham Town were defeated 3-0 thanks to a Vic Horrocks hat-trick in the Southern League.

SATURDAY 5TH NOVEMBER 1932

Joe Johnson and Harry Davies scored as Stoke beat Swansea Town 2-0 in front of 15,268 fans at the Victoria Ground. The Potters were now 11 matches unbeaten at the top of the Second Division table. The good run of results had been completed with the same 11 players throughout except for one change – Stanley Matthews replacing Bobby Liddle – which occurred in one of only two drawn games during the run.

WEDNESDAY 6TH NOVEMBER 1985

Having qualified for the area semi-final of the Full Members' Cup, Stoke took on Oxford United at the Victoria Ground and went out to a solitary goal in the first season of the short-lived competition.

TUESDAY 6TH NOVEMBER 1990

Following relegation to the Third Division, City entered the Freight Rover Trophy. The first tie at the Victoria Ground was a 1-1 draw with Northampton Town with Stoke's goal scored by Paul Barnes. The Potters would not get beyond the group stage thanks to a 3-0 defeat at Mansfield Town in January.

SATURDAY 7TH NOVEMBER 1885

Stoke were taken into extra time for the first time, in the FA Cup first qualifying round, by Crewe Alexandra. Crewe handled the physical strain of the extra 30 minutes better to win 1-0.

TUESDAY 7TH NOVEMBER 1989

Chairman Peter Coates sacked manager Mick Mills "in the interests of Stoke City Football Club" after a string of poor results culminating in a 6-0 reverse at Swindon Town.

SATURDAY 8TH NOVEMBER 1890

The Victoria Athletic Ground was unfit for play so for the Football Alliance game against Crewe Alexandra, and the next one against Bootle, the County Cricket Ground was used. The 2-2 draw was witnessed by a crowd given as 1,000 which is Stoke's joint-lowest home gate ever. Outfield player Hugh Phillips was in goal for this match, and Alf Underwood for the next, as both of Stoke's normal keepers were out injured.

MONDAY 8TH NOVEMBER 1971

After a 1-1 draw at Old Trafford, a crowd of 40,829 turned out for the League Cup fourth round replay against Manchester United. There were few chances created and after extra time the game was still goalless.

SATURDAY 8TH NOVEMBER 1997

Graham Kavanagh with two and Richard Forsyth with the other gave Stoke a 3-0 victory over Wolves at the Britannia Stadium. Chic Bates' side moved up to 8th in the table, but that was as good as it got with only one win in the next 22 attempts.

SATURDAY 9TH NOVEMBER 1946

A crowd of around 26,000 witnessed the goalless draw with Aston Villa. The 1946/47 season saw an average league home attendance of 30,863 which has only been surpassed by the 1947/48 season.

SATURDAY 10TH NOVEMBER 1883

Stoke's first venture into the FA Cup ended in defeat at the hands of Manchester. Teddy Johnson scored in the 2-1 home defeat.

SATURDAY 10TH NOVEMBER 1990

Wigan Athletic were shocking and Mickey Thomas was brilliant as Stoke City won thanks to goals from Wayne Biggins and Mick Kennedy. The victory kept the Potters in third place but a run of two wins in 14 matches ended hopes of an immediate return to the Second Division.

WEDNESDAY 10TH NOVEMBER 1993

Fiorentina visited the Victoria Ground in the Anglo-Italian Cup bringing with them their star name, Gabriel Batistuta. The match finished 0-0 in front of 8,616 fans.

SATURDAY 11TH NOVEMBER 1972

A tremendous game with Southampton at the Victoria Ground ended with honours even after six goals, in front of the lowest home league gate of the season, just 17,772. Stoke goalkeeper John Farmer was having an extended run in the side due to Gordon Banks' eye injury. The Biddulph-born goalkeeper made a total of 185 appearances for City, but occasionally had a dip in confidence which impacted on his performances.

SATURDAY 11TH NOVEMBER 1989

Alan Ball had yet to be given the manager's role on a full-time basis but the players still performed for him by beating Brighton & Hove Albion 3-2 with goals from Carl Beeston, Chris Kamara and Dave Bamber, this time at the right end – his first goal in 11 matches.

SATURDAY 12TH NOVEMBER 1892

Ted 'Jammer' Evans became the first Stoke player to be sent off in a league game. He was dismissed at Everton in front of 12,000 spectators. Stoke's ten men drew the match 2-2 thanks to goals from Jimmy Robertson and Billy Naughton. The season was a good one on the whole and the club finished seventh, their highest league position so far.

SATURDAY 12TH NOVEMBER 1910

Jack Peart and George Turner scored two each – while both Alf Smith and Amos Baddeley grabbed one apiece – as Wrexham were beaten 6-2. George Turner represented Stoke from the formation of the new club in 1908 until he lost a leg whilst fighting for his country in 1918.

SATURDAY 13TH NOVEMBER 1926

Stoke extended their lead over Chesterfield at the top of the Third Division (North) table to four points with a 3-1 victory over promotion rivals Rochdale.

WEDNESDAY 13TH NOVEMBER 1996

The Coca-Cola Cup third round replay at Highbury saw Mike Sheron put City ahead with a quality goal. An exaggerated Denis Bergkamp tumble earned Arsenal a penalty and from that moment they were cruising, running out 5-2 winners. Sheron got the second Potters goal.

SATURDAY 14TH NOVEMBER 1908

The Birmingham League match at Halesowen saw the lowest gate for a Stoke first-team game. Just 200 turned out to see the home win 2-0.

SATURDAY 14TH NOVEMBER 1998

In the FA Cup first round Stoke won at Reading thanks to a Kyle Lightbourne drive. This was the first time City had beaten league opposition away in the FA Cup since 1971.

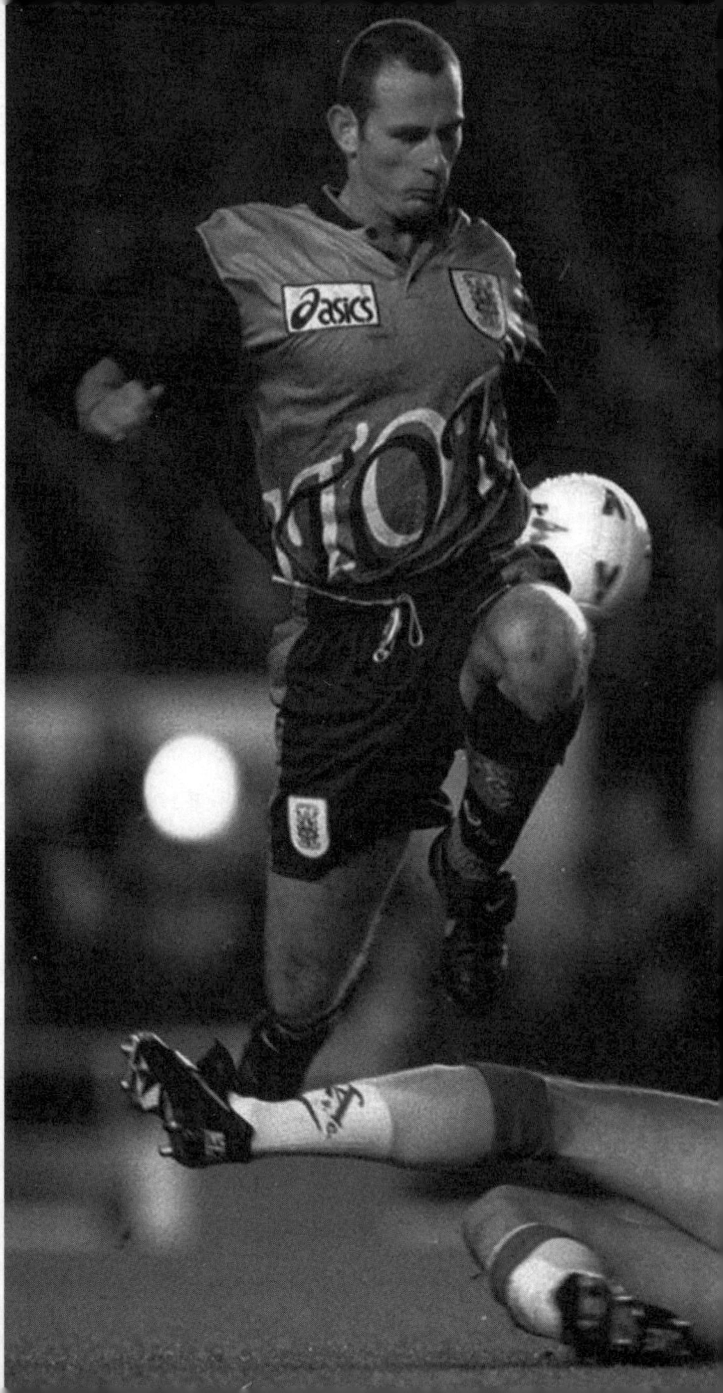

MIKE SHERON IN ACTION AT HIGHBURY IN NOVEMBER 1996

SUNDAY 14TH NOVEMBER 1999

Gary Megson took charge of the Stoke team against Bristol City in the knowledge it would be his last game in charge as the new Icelandic owners wanted their own man in as manager. Megson, who was offered a coaching role, handled himself with dignity as Brian Tinnion equalised five minutes for the Robins from the end to deny him a farewell three points.

SATURDAY 15TH NOVEMBER 1913

A crowd of 4,500 witnessed the visit of Welsh side Barry. Goals from Charlie Revill, Billy Herbert, Dicky Smith and two apiece for Joey Jones and Alf Smith gave Stoke a 7-1 victory. The victory cemented the club's place at the top of the Southern League Division Two table as they had only lost one of the first ten games.

MONDAY 15TH NOVEMBER 1971

The second replay of the League Cup fourth round clash saw Manchester United take the lead for the first time in the tie thanks to George Best. Peter Dobing pulled Stoke City level in the second half and then substitute George Eastham crossed for John Ritchie to head in the winner with only two minutes remaining. The Potters moved into the last eight of the competition to face Bristol Rovers.

MONDAY 15TH NOVEMBER 1999

The Icelandic takeover of Stoke City was completed and a press conference was given by new chairman Gunnar Thor Gislason, Elfar Adalsteinsson and the ex-Bayern Munich player Asgeir Sigurvinsson. It was announced that Gary Megson had been sacked and that he would be replaced by Gudjon Thordarson, the previous Iceland national manager. The whole takeover had been the brain-child of Thordarson which he had thought while on trips to check on the form of defender Larus Sigurdsson.

FRIDAY 16TH NOVEMBER 1962

Lanky defender Steve Bould was born in Stoke. He played over 200 games for City at right-back and centre-half before joining George Graham's Arsenal.

SATURDAY 16TH NOVEMBER 1963

John Ritchie scored a hat-trick in the 4-4 draw with Sheffield Wednesday. The goals took his tally to 15 in nine games as he broke Jack Peart's record for scoring in consecutive games. Only six of these games were in the league with the others being notched in the League Cup.

MONDAY 17TH NOVEMBER 1917

Following their 16-0 defeat at Stoke the previous week, Blackburn Rovers did not show any great signs of improvement as they lost the return fixture 8-1 at Ewood Park. In the first match, Bob Whittingham and George Turner both scored four – with Billy Herbert also claiming a hat-trick – the only time three Stoke players have scored a hat-trick in the same match.

SATURDAY 17TH NOVEMBER 1990

Entered into the first round of the FA Cup for the first time in 64 years, Stoke faced non-league opposition for the first time since Blyth Spartans in 1978. Stoke were rarely troubled by Telford United at the Buck's Head but still needed to rely on a replay to progress to the next round.

WEDNESDAY 18TH NOVEMBER 1936

The last England international match to be staged at the Victoria Ground took place in front of nearly 48,000 fans. Local heroes Freddie Steele and Joe Johnson played for England in the 3-1 win over Ireland. The match was played in Stoke as recognition of the ground improvements which had been made.

SATURDAY 18TH NOVEMBER 1989

Paul Ware achieved the dubious honour of being the first Stoke substitute to be substituted after he was injured at Bournemouth. Despite Vince Hilaire's late goal, Stoke lost 2-1 and sunk to bottom of the Second Division.

SUNDAY 18TH NOVEMBER 2001

Stoke played an away match at the Britannia Stadium as Lewes, their FA Cup first round opponents, switched the tie in order to generate more revenue. City beat the Sussex side 2-0 thanks to goals from Peter Handyside and Brynjar Gunnarsson.

MONDAY 19TH NOVEMBER 1910

In the 1910/11 season Stoke scored a total of 179 goals in all competitions. There were many high scores like the 7-0 win in the FA Cup fourth qualifying round against Worcester City. This came thanks to a hat-trick from Amos Baddeley and two each for Alf Smith and Jack Peart.

SATURDAY 19TH NOVEMBER 1988

A George Berry penalty and a goal from substitute Graham Shaw were enough to beat Hull City 2-1 and lift Stoke to seventh. The game saw the first issue of long-running fanzine, *The Oatcake*.

SATURDAY 20TH NOVEMBER 1937

For the goalless home draw to Sunderland, George Antonio was replaced in the team by debutant Alec Ormston. Ormston was a hunchback who made 192 appearances for the Potters, scoring 30 goals.

WEDNESDAY 20TH NOVEMBER 1974

Tony Waddington looked to solve the team's goalkeeping issues by paying a new world record transfer fee for a goalkeeper of £325,000 to get Peter Shilton from Leicester City. Shilton moved to Nottingham Forest for £270,000 after relegation three years later.

SATURDAY 21ST NOVEMBER 1992

After a run of 12 games unbeaten in the league Stoke hit the top after a 3-1 win in torrential rain at Blackpool, and stayed there all season. Kevin Russell was the hero as Stoke came from behind at Bloomfield Road. 'Rooster' Russell was a much travelled bald-headed winger whose time at City, after joining from Leicester City for £95,000, included seven goals in 56 appearances.

TUESDAY 21ST NOVEMBER 2000

Nuneaton Borough became the latest non-league side to knock Stoke out of the FA Cup. The only goal of the tie came late on in the replay.

SATURDAY 22ND NOVEMBER 1952

Jock Kirton played his last game for Stoke in the 5-1 defeat at Charlton Athletic. He left for Bradford City after making 249 appearances since moving south from Banks o' Dee FC in Aberdeen.

THURSDAY 22ND NOVEMBER 1991

Stoke faced Telford United for the second successive year in the first round of the FA Cup and this time disaster struck. In the replay at Bucks Head, City lost 2-1 despite Carl Beeston's late screamer. The Telford side was managed by former Stokie Gerry Daly and included former player Paul Dyson.

WEDNESDAY 22ND NOVEMBER 1995

Ray Wallace scored the only goal of the game as Sunderland lost their first match in eleven at the Victoria Ground. The game also saw the end of centre-half Vince Overson's Stoke career as Ian Cranson returned from injury to partner Larus Sigurdsson.

TUESDAY 23RD NOVEMBER 1971

Bristol Rovers hosted Stoke in the League Cup quarter-final in front of 33,626. After the epic fourth round tie against Manchester United it was a relief to face the mid-table Third Division side. Jimmy Greenhoff, Denis Smith, Mike Bernard and Terry Conroy took advantage to put Stoke 4-0 ahead before Rovers pulled two back late on.

TUESDAY 23RD NOVEMBER 1999

The excitement and euphoria surrounding the Icelandic takeover of the club and the potential investment in the team continued on to the pitch for Gudjon Thordarson's first game in charge at Wycombe Wanderers. The former Icelandic national team boss had brought in two compatriots already in Einar Thor Danielsson and Sigurdsteinn Gislason. City were rampant, and the travelling supporters delirious, as Graham Kavanagh scored a screamer on 44 minutes and then Danielsson netted a wonder goal just a minute later. The final score was 4-0 to the Potters and surely the club were on their way back?

SATURDAY 24TH NOVEMBER 1962

Stoke drew 1-1 at Cardiff City thanks to a Jackie Mudie goal. In the tunnel at half-time Eddie Clamp butted Colin Webster. This was revenge for Webster's challenge when as a reserve at Manchester United he had broken England prospect George Bourne's leg, some seven years earlier!

TUESDAY 24TH NOVEMBER 1992

The Vale Park mud conspired against Stoke in the FA Cup first round replay. After Lee Sandford had given City the lead, Vale came back through Foyle and Porter before the mud intervened. First Dave Regis' header stuck on the line when he looked certain to equalise, and then the ball stopped again allowing Martin Foyle to beat Stoke keeper Ronnie Sinclair and make it 3-1.

SATURDAY 25TH NOVEMBER 1922

The match away at Blackburn Rovers was abandoned with the score 1-0 in favour of the home side. Stoke's train was delayed and they were forced to take two taxis, one of which broke down. The team arrived 32 minutes late and the match had to be abandoned due to bad light with only four minutes remaining. Stoke won the replayed match 5-1.

SATURDAY 25TH NOVEMBER 1972

West Bromwich Albion hosted the Potters and sent them into the First Division relegation zone with a 2-1 win. Stoke's new claret and blue away kit did not bring them much luck as Tony Brown scored from the penalty spot with six minutes left. Jimmy Greenhoff mis-kicked a chance at the death.

SATURDAY 26TH NOVEMBER 1910

Stoke beat Wolves reserves in the Birmingham League by 6-1, which was the third time in 19 days the Potters had scored six! Jack Peart scored a hat-trick taking his personal tally for those 19 days to eight!

SATURDAY 26TH NOVEMBER 1927

A Maine Road crowd of just under 40,000 witnessed the visit of Stoke in the Second Division. It was not a good day for the Potters as Manchester City won 4-0 and Stoke dropped to sixth.

MONDAY 27TH NOVEMBER 1939

Tony Allen was born in Stoke-on-Trent. The left-back went on to make 473 appearances for the Potters in his 14 years at the club, as well as winning three full England caps.

THURSDAY 28TH NOVEMBER 1895

Tommy Clare became the first player to make 200 appearances for the club in the 4-0 defeat at Nottingham Forest, going on to a total of 251.

SATURDAY 28TH NOVEMBER 1914

During Stoke's championship season in Southern League Division Two, Mid Rhonnda visited the Potteries and were soundly beaten 8-0. Arty Watkins scored his second hat-trick of the season.

SATURDAY 29TH NOVEMBER 1941

Tranmere Rovers suffered their second heavy defeat to Stoke within a week at Prenton Park. The 7-2 victory, with hat-tricks for both Alf Basnett and Tommy Sale, followed on from a 9-0 victory at the Victoria Ground in front of 1,500 spectators.

WEDNESDAY 29TH NOVEMBER 2000

Stoke suffered their record home defeat in the Worthington Cup fourth round match against Liverpool. The Potters had excellent early chances through both Kyle Lightbourne and Peter Thorne, but fell behind to a Christian Ziege goal on six minutes. Gerard Houllier's men then ran riot and scored regularly, including a Robbie Fowler hat-trick., to end up winning 8-0. Most of the 27,000 crowd had long since left when the final whistle went.

SATURDAY 30TH NOVEMBER 1963

Birmingham City were convincingly beaten 4-1 at the Victoria Ground in front of 27,308. John Ritchie scored twice with Peter Dobing and George Kinnell also registering on the score sheet. The average home league attendance in the 1963/64 season was 30,315, making it the third highest in Stoke City's history.

SATURDAY 30TH NOVEMBER 1974

Carl Jayes, in the Leicester City goal, appeared to be unbeatable as Stoke threw everything forward. Eventually the majority of the 29,793 crowd erupted as Denis Smith won the contest with his left foot. Stoke went top of the league, leapfrogging Liverpool who drew at Coventry City.

WEDNESDAY 1st DECEMBER 1888

A 2-1 victory over Blackburn Rovers thanks to strikes from Alf Edge and Bob McSkimming lifted Stoke to eighth place – their highest position in the Football League's first year of the – which was six points ahead of bottom-placed Derby County.

THURSDAY 1st DECEMBER 1938

Peter Dobing, the first person to lift a major trophy for Stoke, was born in Manchester. Dobing signed from Manchester City for £37,500 in 1961 and went on to make 372 appearances, scoring 94 goals in red and white stripes. He had a poor disciplinary record and received a record nine-week ban in 1970, which was not too costly as he had a broken leg at the same time!

SATURDAY 2nd DECEMBER 1911

Crowd trouble marred the 2-0 defeat at home to Queens Park Rangers as a near-riot led to the match being abandoned after 88 minutes. The result was made to stand and Stoke had to pay £4,000 to erect fences around the pitch at the Victoria Ground.

TUESDAY 2nd DECEMBER 1997

Sheffield United took all three points from the Britannia Stadium after Stoke had dominated the game. Peter Thorne's brace put City 2-1 up but the Blades came back to snatch it with Brian Deane's 80th-minute shot.

SATURDAY 3rd DECEMBER 1910

The FA Cup fifth qualifying round 4-0 victory against Lincoln City saw Stoke progress to the first round proper. One of the scorers was Jack Peart who took his tally for the season to 34 goals from 22 games. Unfortunately, he broke his leg two games later and missed the last 35 matches of the season.

SATURDAY 3rd DECEMBER 1921

Jimmy Broad scored four against Crystal Palace in the Second Division clash in front of 9,000 fans at the Victoria Ground. This was the first time any Stoke player had scored four goals in a Football League match.

SATURDAY 3RD DECEMBER 1983

After the 3-1 defeat at Southampton the board's patience finally ran out and Richie Barker was sacked. His conversion during the previous summer to POMO – Position of Maximum Opportunity – had bypassed Stoke's top-class midfield. The direct long-ball style system may have worked for Graham Taylor's Watford, and even for Wolverhampton Wanderers in the 1950s, but it had failed at Stoke. Barker's record as City manager was 30 wins and 47 defeats in 100 league games.

SATURDAY 3RD DECEMBER 2005

At the end of the Championship clash with Queens Park Rangers the visiting goalkeeper Simon Royce was attacked by some home fans who had run on to the pitch.

SATURDAY 4TH DECEMBER 1926

Dick Johnson scored the only goal of the game at Accrington Stanley, in front of 5,000 supporters at Peel Park, as Stoke extended their lead over Nelson at the top of Division Three (North) to six points.

SATURDAY 4TH DECEMBER 1948

John Malkin replaced George Mountford for the trip to Blackpool and Stoke fielded the so-called '£10 team'. That was the total cost of assembling the side, all of whom were locally born except for Frank Mountford, and even he had grown up in the area. After losing the match 2-1, George Mountford returned to the side and the '£10 team' never played together again.

SATURDAY 5TH DECEMBER 1942

George Mountford made his debut in a 3-3 draw at Gresty Road against Crewe Alexandra. He was used mainly as an understudy to Stanley Matthews and died at just 52 years of age in Kidderminster in 1973.

SATURDAY 5TH DECEMBER 1964

Blackpool were the visitors in a First Division contest in which City ran out 4-2 winners. Calvin Palmer netted two on the way to his best total for a season – eight – with the other strikes coming from Dennis Viollet and Peter Dobing in front of 17,360 fans at the Victoria Ground.

MONDAY 6TH DECEMBER 1926

Old Trafford provided the neutral venue for the second replay of the FA Cup first round tie against Rhyl of the Welsh League, after both previous matches had finished 1-1. Only 3,000 turned up to see Stoke embarrassingly defeated 2-1 by the non-league side. Harry Davies grabbed the Potters' goal.

SATURDAY 6TH DECEMBER 2003

After a 3-2 defeat at home to Cardiff City, the Potters found themselves in the bottom three of the First Division – as they were in the previous year – after four defeats in five. The damage was done by former City hero Peter Thorne who scored a hat-trick, although Stoke pulled two back through John Eustace and Ade Akinbiyi.

SATURDAY 7TH DECEMBER 1935

Billy Spencer played his last match for Stoke. He spent ten years playing in either full-back slot, many of them alongside Bob McGrory. In the game, the Potters beat visitors Wolves 4-1 with Tommy Sale and Bobby Liddle both bagging a brace in front of 16,000 spectators.

SATURDAY 7TH DECEMBER 1974

Boothen End hero Jimmy Greenhoff scored a spectacular volley to put Stoke ahead at St Andrew's. City went on to win 3-0 against Birmingham City with Greenhoff notching another against his former club and Ian Moores scoring his first senior goal. The win kept the Potters top of the league for another week.

TUESDAY 7TH DECEMBER 1999

Kyle Lightbourne scored Stoke City's first golden goal winner in the Auto Windscreens Shield first round match at home to Darlington. There were 3,341 there to witness it.

WEDNESDAY 8TH DECEMBER 1971

Stoke appeared to have blown their chances in the first leg of the League Cup semi-final at the Victoria Ground as they went down 2-1 to West Ham United. Peter Dobing gave Stoke the lead inside 15 minutes, but a Geoff Hurst penalty and a Clyde Best goal sent the Hammers contingent in the 36,000 strong crowd home happy.

SATURDAY 8TH DECEMBER 1984

During the horror season of 1984/85, Stoke used five different goalkeepers. For the match at home to Ipswich Town young stopper Stuart Roberts was given his debut. At only 17 years and 258 days old, he became the youngest goalkeeper in the club's history. Stoke dominated the match but two goals in the last ten minutes condemned them to yet another defeat, the tenth in succession.

MONDAY 9TH DECEMBER 1957

Swansea Town visited Stoke in the Second Division and found the King/Kelly strike partnership too hot to handle as George Kelly scored three and Johnny King two in a 6-2 success.

SATURDAY 9TH DECEMBER 1989

Defeat at Oakwell left City with only two wins in 20 games for the season – three in 34 overall – and dumped them to the bottom of the First Division for the rest of the season. Barnsley lifted themselves out of the relegation places with the victory.

TUESDAY 9TH DECEMBER 2003

Struggling Stoke travelled to West Ham United and came away with all three points thanks to a goal from on-loan Frazer Richardson. The victory at Upton Park proved to be the turning point for the season and was inspired by new recruit from Leicester, Gerry Taggart.

SATURDAY 10TH DECEMBER 1966

Harry Burrows hit a hat-trick as Stoke thumped his former team-mates Aston Villa 6-1 at the Victoria Ground. The 20,232 crowd also saw goals from George Eastham, Peter Dobing and Roy Vernon.

SATURDAY 10TH DECEMBER 1983

Bill Asprey took charge for the first time after Richie Barker's dismissal, but Stoke still went down 4-2 at home to David Pleat's Luton Town.

SUNDAY 11TH DECEMBER 1960

Mark Harrison, goalkeeper for both Stoke City and Port Vale amongst others, was born in Derby. Harrison was restricted to just eight appearances for the Potters by the form of Peter Fox.

SATURDAY 11TH DECEMBER 1971

During the 1971/72 season Stoke met Manchester United on seven occasions – including in the First Division – with four draws, two Stoke victories and one United win. The league game at the Victoria Ground was a tight affair with United, top of the league, holding on for a point after Denis Law's header cancelled out John Mahoney's opener.

MONDAY 12TH DECEMBER 1910

The 4-0 win over Walsall in the Southern League Division Two completed a run of eight consecutive home wins for Stoke. During this run the Potters scored 35 goals and conceded just five.

WEDNESDAY 12TH DECEMBER 1973

Manchester United visited the Victoria Ground to play in a testimonial match for Gordon Banks. Stoke had two special guest players that night in Bobby Charlton and Eusebio. The Portuguese gave Stoke the lead but United, inspired by George Best, came back to win 2-1 with goals from Young and Lou Macari.

SATURDAY 12TH DECEMBER 1998

Without the suspended duo of Peter Thorne and Graham Kavanagh, Stoke appeared toothless in the goalless draw with Gillingham. City had only been off top spot for four days, so far, all season.

THURSDAY 13TH DECEMBER 1934

Austria FC, the first continental team to appear at the Victoria Ground during a tour of England, lost to a goal from Harry Davies.

WEDNESDAY 13TH DECEMBER 1967

The League Cup quarter-final against Leeds United ended in a 2-0 defeat at the Victoria Ground in front of nearly 25,000. The result continued Stoke's poor record in cup quarter-finals: the Potters have won only five of seventeen in the FA and League cups.

WEDNESDAY 13TH DECEMBER 1978

Third Division leaders Watford were the visitors in the League Cup quarter-final, which presented Stoke with a fantastic opportunity of reaching the semi-finals. Graham Taylor's side held on to force a replay.

SATURDAY 13TH DECEMBER 2003

Peter Hoekstra put on a masterclass against Reading, scoring all three goals as Stoke lifted themselves away from the relegation places. The popular Dutchman's hat-trick goal came from a cheekily taken penalty.

SATURDAY 14TH DECEMBER 1895

Goals from Teddy Sandland and Joe Schofield could not prevent Stoke going down to a crushing 7-2 defeat at the hands of Everton at Goodison Park in front of a large 10,000 crowd.

MONDAY 14TH DECEMBER 1981

Stoke City's former Mansfield Town and Sunderland winger, Liam Lawrence, was born in Retford, Nottinghamshire. Lawrence was Player of the Season in 2007/08 as City won promotion to the Premiership.

SATURDAY 15TH DECEMBER 1923

Harry Sellars signed from Ledgate Park and went on to make 394 appearances for the Potters. Harry's son, Johnny, also had a lengthy career with Stoke – playing in more games than his father – until being forced to retire due to an eye injury in 1959. This ended a 36-year association between the Sellars family and Stoke City Football Club.

WEDNESDAY 15TH DECEMBER 1971

With away goals not counting double, John Ritchie's 72nd-minute strike in the second leg at Upton Park appeared to have forced the League Cup semi-final against West Ham United into a replay. The drama unfolded with only a couple of minutes left as Mike Pejic and Gordon Banks were involved in a mix up which resulted in the latter bringing down Harry Redknapp for a penalty. Geoff Hurst blasted the resultant spot-kick but the England man somehow got to it to force the replay.

WEDNESDAY 15TH DECEMBER 1982

Mark Chamberlain made his England debut versus Luxembourg at Wembley Stadium, coming on as a substitute for Steve Coppell. The result was never in doubt and England won 9-0. Chamberlain got the sixth of the goals just minutes after coming on to the field. This was the last England goal to be scored by a Stoke City player.

SATURDAY 15TH DECEMBER 2001

Brynjar Gunnarsson scored twice as Stoke comfortably beat Lawrie Sanchez's Wycombe Wanderers 5-1 at the Britannia Stadium. Andy Cooke, Marc Goodfellow and Chris Iwelumo got the others goals. The win put City top of Division Two for the first time in 2001/02.

SATURDAY 16TH DECEMBER 1972

Geoff Hurst returned to Upton Park as a Stoke City player – and scored – but ended up on the losing side as West Ham United came back to win 3-2. John Ritchie grabbed Stoke's second at the death. World Cup hat-trick hero Hurst joined the Potters from the Hammers in 1972 and scored 37 goals in 128 appearances.

SATURDAY 16TH DECEMBER 1978

Peter Fox made his debut in goal for Stoke and did not have too taxing an afternoon as City beat Wrexham 3-0 in front of 18,358.

SATURDAY 17TH DECEMBER 1955

Johnny King (2), Andy Graver, Tim Coleman and Frank Bowyer were the scorers as Stoke thrashed Doncaster Rovers 5-2 at the Victoria Ground in the Second Division.

SATURDAY 17TH DECEMBER 1960

Johnny King grabbed his first hat-trick for five years as Stoke thrashed Plymouth Argyle 9-0. Don Ratcliffe and Bill Asprey scored two each whilst Dennis Wilshaw, and a Fincham own goal, completed the rout. A poor Victoria Ground crowd of 6,479 were there to witness the rout.

WEDNESDAY 18TH DECEMBER 1991

Stoke met the holders Birmingham City in the group stages of the Autoglass Trophy and won 3-1 thanks to Paul Barnes, Mark Stein and Paul Ware. This result, coupled with a previous success at Walsall, saw City qualify for round one proper of the competition.

SATURDAY 18TH DECEMBER 1999

Despite being cynically targeted by the Bristol Rovers defence, Kevin Keen scored the first goal – but Stoke could not extend the lead and the Pirates snatched a 2-1 win with two late goals.

SATURDAY 19TH DECEMBER 1942

Almost 12 months after suffering an 8-0 defeat at Stoke, Walsall came back to the Victoria Ground for more of the same. This time, witnessed by 5,100 supporters, City won 7-1 with Frank Mountford (2), George Mountford, Alf Basnett, Tommy Sale, Bobby Liddle and a Male own goal making up the scoring. A week previously, and a week later, Stoke beat Crewe Alexandra twice by a 6-1 scoreline.

SATURDAY 19TH DECEMBER 1998

Andy Rammell scored for Walsall to knock Stoke off the top of Nationwide Division Two and start a depressing slide down the table.

SATURDAY 20TH DECEMBER 1947

Freddie Steele and Johnny Sellars were the scorers as Stoke beat Bolton Wanderers at the Victoria Ground in front of 23,404 spectators. The 1947/48 season saw the highest average league home gate in the club's history with an average crowd of 31,099, beating the previous season's record.

SATURDAY 20TH DECEMBER 2003

Stoke won at Vicarage Road thanks to two goals from Ade Akinbiyi and one from Gerry Taggart. Watford could only get a consolation goal in front of 13,736. Akinbiyi resurrected his career at City after he had become a bit of a laughing stock in some quarters. Ade scored a total of 19 goals in 67 outings for Stoke before moving to Burnley.

SATURDAY 21ST DECEMBER 1918

Bob Whittingham and George Brown both scored hat-tricks in the 7-1 home victory against Bolton Wanderers. Charlie Parker struck the other. Both were guest players but ended as the top two scorers for the season.

SUNDAY 21ST DECEMBER 1986

After being beaten 6-2 the previous season, Leeds United goalkeeper Mervyn Day had vowed he was not going to concede six this time: instead he conceded seven! Stoke ran riot with Nicky Morgan claiming a hat-trick and the other goals coming from Carl Saunders, Lee Dixon, Tony Ford and Tony 'Zico' Kelly.

SATURDAY 22ND DECEMBER 1934

A crowd of only 4,037 at Leeds Road in Huddersfield witnessed Stoke's 4-1 victory in the First Division. There were two goals from Tommy Sale as well as goals from Harry Davies and Bobby Liddle, but none from debutant Freddie Steele. This was not a sign of things to come as 'Nobby' went on to become one of the greatest goalscorers in the club's history. His 16-year career with the Potters yielded a record total of 140 league goals, a record 19 in the FA Cup and 81 in wartime football. These 240 goals came in only 346 first-team matches and included 24 hat-tricks. Capped six times by England – it would have been more but for the war – Steele announced his retirement aged 23 when the war broke out. After psychiatric treatment he scored ten times in the next five games!

SATURDAY 22ND DECEMBER 2007

Jamaican international Ricardo Fuller scored a hat-trick, his first for Stoke, against league leaders West Bromwich Albion to give Stoke a 3-1 win. The Albion's record against Stoke is poor, with no win in their last 17 visits stretching back to 1982/83, and only two wins in the last 25 games against the Potters, home or away.

MONDAY 23RD DECEMBER 1889

Stoke beat Burnley 2-1 with Jimmy Sayer and Billy Hendry scoring. During the match Bob McCormick badly injured his breast bone and at the final whistle the crowd invaded the pitch. Burnley appealed claiming that their players had been intimidated. The appeal was upheld and the Clarets won the replayed match 4-3.

SATURDAY 23RD DECEMBER 2006

Liam Lawrence – the right-winger who was on loan from Sunderland but signed permanently the following January – scored the only goal as Stoke took all three points against Ipswich Town at Portman Road. The result left City in fourth place in the Championship and eyeing a possible play-off spot.

SATURDAY 24TH DECEMBER 1892

The Potters lost by the only goal away to Derby County thanks to an error by their goalkeeper Billy Rowley. Rowley was a controversial figure who was both a player and manager at Stoke.

SATURDAY 24th DECEMBER 1960

Dennis Wilshaw grabbed a brace as Stoke City drew 2-2 with Huddersfield Town in the Second Division. The Potters would play the return match with the Terriers on Boxing Day, and again honours would be even after a 0-0 draw.

SATURDAY 25th DECEMBER 1909

Christmas Day was a happy occasion for Stoke as they ran out 7-1 winners at Burton United in the Southern League. Amos Baddeley scored five to take his tally for the season in all competitions to 17. In the return match two days later Stoke ran out 5-0 winners with Baddeley again on the score sheet.

FRIDAY 25th DECEMBER 1931

Tom Mather was able to name the same line-up for the 15th consecutive match, a record for the club. The team was: Arthur Lewis, Bob McGrory, Arthur Beachill, Billy Robertson, Arthur Turner, Harry Sellars, Bobby Liddle, Walter Bussey, Joe Mawson, Tommy Sale and Bobby Archibald. Nottingham Forest were beaten 2-1, with Sale getting a brace.

WEDNESDAY 25th DECEMBER 1940

During the Second World War, Stoke received a 7-2 hiding from Mansfield Town in the Southern Regional League in front of 3,450 at Field Mill.

SATURDAY 25th DECEMBER 1954

Johnny King gave the Stoke City fans an extra Christmas present by scoring a hat-trick against Bury in the Potters' 3-2 success. A crowd of 18,312 were at the Victoria Ground to witness the feat.

WEDNESDAY 26th DECEMBER 1984

Stoke City registered only their second victory of the season against second-placed Manchester United. A season's best crowd of 21,013 saw the Potters turn things around in the last 20 minutes with an Ian Painter penalty and a Carl Saunders finish from a corner, after Frank Stapleton had put United ahead.

MONDAY 26TH DECEMBER 1988

Over 24,000 fans packed the Victoria Ground for the visit of Manchester City. New signings John Butler and Dave Bamber had an instant impact as Stoke ran out 3-1 winners after falling behind. The football inflatable craze was at its height and Manchester City had adopted the banana whilst Stoke fans waved around inflatable Pink Panthers!

TUESDAY 26TH DECEMBER 1989

Lee Sandford made his debut for the Potters having driven through the night to sign for Alan Ball's Potters from Portsmouth. Sandford and fellow debutant Tony Ellis made a difference as City beat Newcastle United 2-1, coming from behind with a Wayne Biggins finish and a Carl Beeston pile-driver in the last minute. Sandford left for Sheffield United in 1996 for £500,000 after seven years service and 324 appearances.

WEDNESDAY 26TH DECEMBER 2007

Liam Lawrence scored a dramatic hat-trick to earn Stoke a point at Barnsley. The hat-trick included two penalties, the second of which was scored eight minutes into injury time!

SATURDAY 27TH DECEMBER 1947

A crowd of 47,409 turned out for the visit of Blackpool, and their new signing Stanley Matthews. This was Stoke's second-highest home gate for a league match, which finished 1-1 with Tommy Kiernan scoring for the Potters.

TUESDAY 27TH DECEMBER 1966

A Harry Burrows double saw Stoke City beat Burnley 4-3 to go third in the First Division, having already beaten them 2-0 at Turf Moor the day before. Despite the promise of this season, four wins in the last 19 matches consigned Stoke to mid-table.

SATURDAY 28TH DECEMBER 1940

The wartime game away to Walsall saw long-serving goalkeeper Dennis Herod make his debut in place of Bridges. The game did not go well for the youngster as Stoke went down 5-1, but it did not stop his career from flourishing afterwards and he stayed at City for another 13 years.

FRIDAY 28TH DECEMBER 1962

The winter of 1962/63 was particularly harsh. The 2-1 win over Rotherham United in December was the last competitive match for nine weeks until 2nd March when Stoke took on Walsall, winning 3-0 thanks to a Jackie Mudie hat-trick.

MONDAY 28TH DECEMBER 1964

Carl Saunders was born in Marston Green in Warwickshire. Carl was a product of the youth system at Stoke and scored 31 goals in 192 games for the club. Mainly used as a striker, Saunders was so adaptable and was one of only three players to wear every outfield shirt for the club – in the days before squad numbers – along with Eric Skeels and Paul Ware.

SATURDAY 29TH DECEMBER 2001

City came away from Huddersfield Town with a good point after a goalless draw. The defensive strength was aided by the return from a one-match ban of Siarhei Shtaniuk, the big Belarussian defender, who played 95 times for Stoke.

SATURDAY 29TH DECEMBER 2007

After waiting all season for his chance to make an impression between the sticks, Russell Hoult lasted 82 minutes before receiving his marching orders for bringing down Sylvan Ebanks-Blake, during the 2-2 draw at Plymouth Argyle. Steve Simonsen reclaimed the jersey and Hoult departed for Notts County at the end of the season.

THURSDAY 30TH DECEMBER 1937

Gordon Banks was born in Sheffield. After starting his career at Chesterfield, Banks signed for Stoke from Leicester City for £52,000 in 1967 as Peter Shilton ousted him from the Foxes first team, and went on to make nearly 250 appearances for the Potters. 'Banks of England' played 73 times for his country – 36 whilst at Stoke – and was hailed as the greatest goalkeeper of all time. He earned a World Cup winner's medal, became an OBE, was voted Footballer of the Year in 1972, and succeeded Sir Stanley Matthews as Life President of Stoke City in 2001.

SATURDAY 31st DECEMBER 1898

A good crowd of around 10,000 came to see Stoke take on Aston Villa. Goals from Joe Turner, John Kennedy and Willie Maxwell sealed a 3-0 win for the Potters.

FRIDAY 31st DECEMBER 1920

Harry Howell made his test match debut for England in the Ashes match at the MCG in Melbourne. Harry, who took three wickets in the contest, played football for Crewe Alexandra, Wolverhampton Wanderers and Manchester United. During the First World War he guested for Stoke, playing 57 games and scoring 42 goals. He went on to appear in four more test matches before dying, aged only 41, in 1932.